The Pen and the Bell

The Pen and the Bell

Mindful Writing in a Busy World

Brenda Miller and Holly J. Hughes

Holly J. Hughes

For Bev—
with gratitude for your—and Sophie's—
presence in our lives... ☺
May these words inspire
your own—so glad you
could join us today...

Holly
May 17, 2014

Skinner House Books
Boston

www.skinnerhouse.org

Printed in the United States

Cover design by Kathryn Sky-Peck
Text design by Suzanne Morgan
Cover art, *Brushstroke 5* by Jim Ballard, used with permission.
Photo of Brenda Miller by Anita K. Boyle
Photo of Holly J. Hughes by Isolde Pierce

print ISBN: 978-1-55896-653-6
eBook ISBN: 978-1-55896-654-3

6 5 4 3 2
15 14 13

Library of Congress Cataloging-in-Publication Data

Miller, Brenda, 1959-
   The pen and the bell : mindful writing in a busy world / Brenda Miller and Holly J. Hughes.
      p. cm.
   Includes bibliographical references.
   ISBN 978-1-55896-653-6 (pbk. : alk. paper) ± ISBN 978-1-55896-654-3 (ebook)
1. Authorship—Psychological aspects. I. Hughes, Holly J. II. Title.
PN171.P83M54 2012
808'.02019--dc23
                              2011043003

Copyright acknowledgments appear on page 201.

To Fox and Abbe, who remind us every day how to be in this world

Contents

Foreword by Norman Fischer   ix
Preface   xiii
Ways to Use This Book   xix

One   Sitting Down and Waking Up   1
Two   Details, Details, Details   11
Three   Lectio Divina   21
Four   Opening the Senses   29
Five   Preparation Is Everything   37
Six   Practice, Practice, Practice   43
Seven   Contemplation at Work   51
Eight   The Moments in Between   65
Nine   Reviving Spiritual Traditions   73
Ten   Eating as Contemplative Practice   81
Eleven   On Gratitude   91
Twelve   Travel as Contemplative Practice   101
Thirteen   Encounters with the Wild   115
Fourteen   Our Animal Companions   127
Fifteen   Dwelling in Our Bodies   135
Sixteen   Responding to Art   145
Seventeen   Allowing Emptiness   153
Eighteen   On Mortality   163
Nineteen   Befriending Solitude and Grief   173
Twenty   Balancing Contemplation and Action   181

A Final Offering   191
Bibliography   193

Foreword

I've devoted my adult life mostly to doing nothing. That's a provocative way of saying that since my youth I've been a Zen priest, devoted to *zazen*, or Zen sitting meditation—a practice in which one sits quietly doing little more than experiencing life as it flows by, moment by moment, breath by breath. Zazen has been one important way for me to stay in touch with the mystery of being a person—and maybe even to make that mystery deeper and darker, to continually remind myself of the strangeness that's always been there, if I will only stay still long enough to feel it. So I am forever recommending meditation practice to others. It seems to me we all need it. Not only to slow down our minds and get a break from our rushing around. But also to appreciate the depth of what we are—to return to amazement at the predicament and delight of being human together in this colorful, fleeting world.

But somehow, for me, zazen has not been enough. I'm not complaining—zazen serves many perfectly well all by itself. Yet, for some reason, writing has always been a necessity for me as well. In the pages that follow, Brenda Miller mentions that she feels out of sorts if a few weeks go by and she hasn't written. I'm like that too. As my dear friend and fellow Zen priest Philip Whalen used to exclaim, with some exasperation, "I got a terrible writing habit!"

In Zen circles, literature is a standing joke, something one feels the need to (if humorously) apologize for. Nevertheless, many Zen people have been writers —in fact, almost all of them have written poems to express and celebrate their understanding (and non-understanding) of life. In Japan especially, expression of all sorts has been an important part of Zen practice, and this is one of that culture's great treasures. The art of making a cup of tea, offering a flower, blowing a simple note on a flute, or making a bold stroke of black ink on a scrap of paper are all Zen expressions that say, "This is our life, this present, fleeting, beautiful, terrible moment we will never be able to fathom."

But writing is something else again. We humans uniquely live in language. Accessing the mystery of our being through language has always been a crucial part of our nature. As Holly Hughes and Brenda Miller make clear in this book, language is essentially a spiritual practice—a practice perhaps more available to us today than meditation, prayer, or anything else. Writing was at one time an esoteric practice for specialists. When I was an aspiring adolescent writer, I looked up to writers as rare individuals, the anointed ones, literary lions whose fame and fortune was often accompanied by the suffering that only genius enjoys. Those days are gone. In our time, writing, as magical as ever, is available to everyone. Texts can be better or worse, more or less praised or popular, but the process of writing itself—writing as discovery, writing as spiritual practice— is now open to any of us who feel the call.

Which brings me to the book you now have in your hands. Strictly speaking, this isn't a book—it's a beautiful, quiet path into the deep woods of contemplative practice through the medium of the written word. Yes, reading its chapters will delight you. Yes, listening to these two wise women talk quietly about their lives and their writing process is a sweet and effortless reading experience that will make you feel as if you are sitting across from them, a cup of tea in front of you, hearing the measure and lilt of their kindly, honest voices. But the real crux of this book/path isn't their words—it's yours. Each chapter concludes with two sets of exercises—contemplative (the bell) and writing (the pen). The contemplative practices will bring you back to quiet, to yourself. And the writing practices will bring you to your senses, to your intimate, inmost experience. Simply reading this text as if it were a book won't nearly be enough. You must do the exercises, you must spend time, plenty of time, maybe years, and you must, even better, spend some of that time with others—writing together, reading together, talking together about what you've read and written. This will, inevitably, bring you to a much deeper appreciation of the mystery you are, that you will never give up trying to understand. Thank you, Holly and Brenda, for so thoughtfully facilitating this endless journey.

Norman Fischer
author of *Sailing Home: Using the Wisdom of Homer's* Odyssey *to Navigate Life's Perils and Pitfalls*

Preface

A certain day became a presence to me;
there it was, confronting me—a sky, air, light:
a being. And before it started to descend
from the height of noon, it leaned over
and struck my shoulder as if with
the flat of a sword, granting me
honor and a task. The day's blow
rang out, metallic—or it was I, a bell awakened,
and what I heard was my whole self
saying and singing what it knew: *I can.*

—Denise Levertov, "Variation on a Theme by Rilke"

Denise Levertov's poem describes a state of mind many of us would love to achieve in our daily lives. Wouldn't it be wonderful to feel that each day we're granted an "honor and a task," and each day to know that we can easily do this work—with pleasure, focus, and joy? For those of us who love to write—or think we *might* love to write if we could simply find the time to do it—this honor and task could be sitting down with our minds wide open, our pens and notebooks and computers at the ready, to articulate our perceptions as accurately and as beautifully as we can. In this way, writing serves a purpose greater than the product alone; it becomes a spiritual practice, a way to connect ourselves to that "presence," however it manifests in our lives.

This book is about how to create space for writing in a world crowded with so many distractions. It's about how many of us long to be "a bell awakened," and yet how difficult it can be to achieve that state in the face of our massive to-do lists. It's about gaining access to our deeper selves in the workaday world, and bringing forth this authentic self in our writing.

The *Pen* in our title refers to the writing process; the *Bell* refers to those things that can support the writing process, the tools that can help us to stop a moment and settle down in a contemplative frame of mind to just listen, to take in as much as we can. In mindfulness practice, a little bell is rung often to remind us to stop, breathe, listen. In life, these bells can be anything we choose: perhaps the bells we hear in a meditation room or a place of worship, but also the bells of everyday life—the call of a bird, the laugh of a child, or a familiar voice on the radio. In this book, we provide you with stories, readings, and writing prompts that address both the pen and the bell: We offer many suggestions for both everyday writing practices and contemplative practices—some of which take only a few minutes— and we give you examples of readings that illustrate both processes.

As writers who have incorporated spirituality as a part of our lives, we have found that writing, in and of itself, can be a powerful form of contemplation: Writing can focus us, center us, slow us down, and allow us to simply observe as clearly as possible. Rabbi Ruth Sohn has defined spirituality as "a search for the affirmation and cultivation of the inner life. . . . It is the desire to learn to be more mindful, to slow down and live more deeply each and every moment. It is the desire to be more tuned in to the present, to be more open, more aware and appreciative of what we have, here, right now." We believe that writing fits perfectly into that definition of spiritual practice and can be a rich, active form of paying attention to the self and the world.

We also believe that contemplative practice can *strengthen* one's writing; the two work synergistically to support and reinforce each other. We hope that by creating more contemplative space in your life, you will also naturally find more detailed, original material to draw upon for your writing. You will become skilled at paying attention, and so will notice more of the sensory details of the world; these details will infuse your writing and evoke rich meaning. You might also find yourself able to tap into a deeper reservoir of memory for your stories, and do so without judgment or other negative emotions that can get in the way. You will become more trusting of your intuition, and might be able to train yourself to write promising material in just a few minutes a day. We want to help you find the space for both contemplation and writing within the realities of day-to-day life, to make room for whatever connects you to your own creativity.

The two of us—Holly and Brenda—created this book out of a shared concern that the pace of life for most people is spiraling out of control, leaving less and less space for "unproductive" time: the gestation period, the quiet musings. We saw the stress in our students and in our fellow writers getting in the way of what was most important to them. So we spent a year writing letters to one another about the twin subjects of writing and contemplation, about how these processes have manifested and evolved in our own lives. And the most wonderful thing happened: the letter writing, for both of us, became a deep and rich practice. The letters took on their own life, showed us details or memories we never would have found otherwise, because the simple words—"Dear Holly," "Dear Brenda"—became our bells of mindfulness. And we had each other as an audience to these thoughts, a listening ear that helped us settle down.

We then shaped this book around the topics we discovered, keeping most of our stories as a way to provide personal examples of how these concepts play out in real life. Some chapters focus more on contemplation, some more on writing. But in every chapter you'll hear both our voices speaking side by side as we describe our struggles to make time for reflection and writing in a world filled with a thousand interruptions, and share our insights for achieving that goal.

In the process, we came to fully understand that all those interruptions are really life itself, not something apart from life. Contemplation and writing do not happen only in quiet places, in sanctified rooms. In fact, we need to be in contact with the world, to feel ourselves in dialogue with our ordinary lives, rather than resisting them. If we train ourselves, we'll see that our writing material, and our contemplative state of mind, can be found anywhere: in the Volkswagen repair shop, at the doctor's office, in a traffic jam, at PetSmart. Through our personal narratives—and through the readings and exercises—we hope to guide you in finding the elusive still point in your own busy life, and we encourage you to articulate what you hear once the clamor ceases.

At the moment, as we write this preface to you, we are lucky enough to work in a quiet place, where the day begins with the ringing whistle of red-winged blackbirds in the marsh and ends with great horned owls calling us to pay attention for just one more minute before the day is done. Here, we really feel ourselves imbued with Levertov's mantra: *I can.* We pulled a book of Levertov's poems off the shelf at dawn, opened it serendipitously to this message that reminded us why we are here, what our "honor and task" might be for today. Levertov wrote her poem in dialogue with the poet Rilke, and so it seems even more fitting as our opening bell. Because through writing the stories that make up this book, inspired and supported by one another, we realized that we are—all of us—truly writing together, in dialogue with one another, even in the midst of stillness and solitude.

We invite you to read this book in whatever ways work for you. You can read it from beginning to end, noticing the way our conversation unfolds, or you can dip into it at random, drawn by whatever topic captures your eye. We hope your copy of the book becomes battered and well worn, evidence of tactile use in practical ways. Whatever way you choose to use *The Pen and the Bell*, we hope that you will find yourself whispering *I can, I can, I can* when you next sit down to write.

Brenda Miller and Holly J. Hughes
Meadow House, Whidbey Island

Ways to Use This Book

We hope this book will be both useful and versatile. Here are some ways you can approach your reading:

Writing as a Contemplative Practice

You can work through this book using our prompts and readings to develop or supplement a spiritual practice through writing. With this approach, you are not striving for a polished end result in your writing; you will be enjoying the practice itself: learning how to slow down, to breathe, to observe yourself and the world around you. You'll take time for yourself and your creativity, and you'll build more spaciousness into your life.

Improving Your Writing through Contemplative Practice

You can use this book to improve your writing, perhaps with a goal in mind. Practice for its own sake is still at the heart of all the writing prompts, but you will find many tips for strengthening your writing through honing your powers of observation, using sensory details, and focusing on small concrete images in order to get at larger questions. You will find many suggestions for material to work with in your writing, giving you an abundant storehouse of places to begin.

Combining Spiritual Practice and Writing Practice

Since the contemplative and the instructional aspects of this book are inter-twined, you can take both approaches described above. As we state in the pref-ace, we believe writing and contemplative practice can support and reinforce each other. Some weeks you may find yourself drawn to one aspect more than the other. Or perhaps you will wish to concentrate on improving your writing once you have more material.

Structuring Your Writing Practice

You may find it useful to structure your writing practice around the chapters in this book, choosing to do one chapter a week (or even one each month). In this way you will find that your time to write increases, since you will have created the space for it in your schedule, and will have guidance on what to do with this focused time.

Practicing Alone or with Others

This book works equally well as a solitary practice or as part of a writing, read-ing, spirituality, or meditation group. You can choose to work through one or two chapters a month, coming together to share your work. We envision circles of writers coming together, trying the same writing and contemplation exercises and sharing the results. You don't even need to do this in person; since many of us live our lives online, an online writing group would work beautifully, too.

Writing Letters as a Way to Practice

As we describe in the preface, shaping your writing through correspondence can be a powerful way to practice both writing and contemplation. You might consider doing all of your practice by writing in the form of letters: either to one person or several. This will give you motivation, and once it becomes a habit to begin your writing with "Dear ____," this phrase will become a powerful mindfulness bell, setting you immediately in the frame of mind to write.

One

Sitting Down and Waking Up

> . . . Except
> for paying attention, what else
> is continual prayer?
> —Samuel Green, *The Grace of Necessity*

Brenda

A long time ago, before I even knew how to be a writer, I attended a writers' workshop with Terry Tempest Williams in Missoula, Montana. My fellow students and I sat ourselves in a small circle, nodding shyly to one another as we waited for our teacher to arrive. When Terry breezed into the room, wafting a scent of sage, she immediately pulled from her bag a clay whistle in the shape of a turtle. She blew into the whistle three times—three quick sharp blasts that cut through our nervousness, our wish to be elsewhere. At that moment, before Terry had even said a word, we had learned something: how to be *really* here, right now, ready to learn, ready to write.

I remember little else of that workshop: not what we discussed, not what we wrote. I'm sure I came away with some concrete tools to use. But I *do* remember Terry sitting next to me in the circle, her long skirt brushing her calves. I remember her presence, the way she shifted from being somewhere else, busy and hurried, to being fully *here*, in that room, the whistling object in her hand.

Now, decades later, I've learned that becoming truly present is both the hardest and the most necessary thing for me to do—both in life and in writing.

In my small home, I try to keep my upstairs attic loft reserved for reading, writing, and sometimes—when I can remember to do it—meditation. My dog, Abbe, often joins me there and makes her nest in the blanket next to me, digging with her paws until the blanket's messy enough to be comfortable. She flops down with a human-like sigh. Only when she is settled do I settle, adjusting myself on the cushion before ringing my little bell. And to do so, I have to take up the only implement handy: a pen. Abbe has gnawed the bell's wooden striker beyond recognition, so I use an ordinary Bic ballpoint to tap against the bell before beginning my few minutes of sitting meditation. Like Terry's whistle, this bell calls me to attention—to the attentive stance necessary for writing.

The word *contemplation* literally means "in the temple," and when we reserve places for contemplative activities we sanctify them in some way. For me, the upstairs can feel like a different world altogether, removed from the quiet bedlam going on downstairs: all the email, the mail, the newspaper, the television, the blogs I simply must read, the student papers, the to-do list. All of them clamor like toddlers for constant attention, though my attention is not really needed there, not every moment of the day. My attention is more acutely needed here, upstairs.

When life gets busy, I sometimes don't make it up here at all. I often don't realize it until I feel myself spiraling downward into a familiar depression. If I'm lucky, it will hit me: *Well, of course, you haven't been upstairs in two weeks!* So I'll climb the stairs to find the room quietly waiting for me, unchanged (except for more dust!), the cushion sitting still on the rug, the rumpled dog blanket in position next to it. The dog might be there, too, looking up with inquiring eyes, as if to say, *Where have you been?* And I remember, once again, that if there's anything I think I've lost, I just need to go upstairs to find it.

Writing too can be a meditation, a time when we simply allow ourselves to observe and become curious about where those observations lead us. We allow the noise of the day to subside in order to hear a deeper voice—one that is always present but often muted—and sometimes all it takes is a simple "call to attention" to bring this voice forward.

This call doesn't need to come from a fancy meditation bell or expensive equipment ordered from catalogs. It might be as simple as really tasting those first few sips of your morning coffee before reading the paper or listening to the radio. Or taking just a minute to study the branches of a tree outside your window, seeing how they change in small increments day to day. Or it might be something as simple as tapping an ordinary pen against your cereal bowl, finding something—anything—that resonates to begin your day with a subtle, vibrant call to attention.

Coming to attention is what writing is all about. We observe and take in what the world offers at every turn. Only by paying attention can we offer that world back to our readers, now transformed through our authentic voices. As Laraine Herring says in *Writing Begins with the Breath,* "Writers struggle to find their voices because they struggle with the process of listening. When we as writers talk about finding our voices, we mean: What do I sound like when there is nothing and no one else speaking? What do I have to say once the distractions of my life are stilled?" Writing begins with listening, and listening can begin with the simplest bell of mindfulness, inviting you to stop for a moment and breathe.

When you're working this way—quieting down, really paying attention— you'll begin to feel like a genius. Really! The derivation of the word *genius* means a god who protects the headwaters, the originating source of a fresh spring. So, to be a genius means really to be *original,* in every sense of the word: returning to your origin, to your "upstairs," to that quiet space where your true voice awaits.

Holly

Paying attention became a practice for me when I fished salmon commercially for eight years in Alaska. While fishing was the hardest physical work I've done, there were also long stretches of time for contemplation: sailing north in the spring when the days were long and we could run twenty hours, or after we'd set the green, dripping gillnet off the stern of our thirty-three-foot boat and waited for it to fill with silver salmon. The time between bursts of activity was filled with reading, writing, and navigating, which I later came to understand as my own version of mindfulness practice.

I loved the way fishing grounded me firmly in the moment with whatever needed attention: twenty sleek king salmon waiting to be cleaned, a storm gathering, a ten-hour run back to town through the red and green lights of Wrangell Narrows. We needed to pay attention to the way the wind veered out of the southwest and picked up to forty knots. We needed to pay attention to the odd clatter in the diesel engine when we ran it at six hundred rpms. I needed to notice my body—my stomach turning queasy as we rounded the cape and headed out into open waters.

The Zen master Thich Nhat Hanh became my mentor in the practice of paying attention. On my fishing trips, I stashed one of his books next to my bunk, and read it each night after wheel watch. At last, I could put a name to what I'd come to call "wheel-watch mind": mindfulness practice. *Breathing in, I breathe in the world; breathing out, I release my thoughts.* Again and again, I repeated this phrase until it seemed true: that I could pour my mind out onto the horizon, that I could become as empty and light as the hollow bones we found littering the beach when we went ashore.

No wonder, then, that when I remember this my mind feels bigger, for the word *attention* comes from the Latin *attendere*, meaning "to stretch, especially the mind." We attend to that which we give our attention. We often use this word to refer to errands—we attend to details, to our affairs—but *attending to* is perhaps most significantly a sacred act. We attend to the sick, the bereaved, the dying. When I attend to all the details of my life in this way, with focused attention, I am connected both to myself and to the world outside my window.

Washington poet Samuel Green calls these daily observations "small noticings"; these are the details that make our writing come alive, the details that William Blake called "bright particulars." In Green's book *The Grace of Necessity*, he includes a section called "Daily Practice," where he includes a short poem for each day (with the date as the title), usually based on a single image. Here's an example of a simple observation—an early-blooming plum—that blossoms into a lovely metaphor:

> The one early plum
> in the orchard has bloomed,
> the flower girl gone to school
> in the dress that she wore
> to the wedding.

This practice keeps the poet alert to the daily events in the natural world, and these images can then reflect our human lives. Green's sequence of "small noticings" written the week of September 11, 2001, are especially powerful because they do this so well. Here's one I admire because, although he wrote it two days before September 11, it seems prescient:

> A nuthatch slams into the bay
> window. The ledge catches her,
> keeps her from the cat's mouth.

but she stays there, stunned, caught
by the betrayal of air turned suddenly
solid. How could she ever move
past this moment without the grace
of necessity? How could any of us?

His haunting questions, even if written before the event, resonate: "How could she ever move/past this moment without the grace/of necessity? How could any of us?" In his daily noticing on September 11, he lets a simple observation of fallen plums carry the weight of this tragedy:

The rain-split plums
have been falling, the ground
so littered now that numbers
no longer have any meaning.

Of course, the fallen plums here can be viewed as human lives, so many now "that numbers / no longer have any meaning." Again, by noticing what's around him—the plums littering the ground—the poet is able to convey a powerful message at a time when so many of us were rendered speechless. Green admits, "I was LOOKING for parallel details, some noticing that would stand for the event, and the plums were perfect. I think there are at least two ways to approach this: one is to know what you're looking for beforehand; the second is just to notice, begin with the details, and discover in that process some meaning that expands beyond the moment."

This practice serves Green well in writing about a devastating emotional event, but he employs it equally well in writing about what we see each day. I, too, find that this daily practice of observation—sometimes on a walk, sometimes just looking at what's outside the window of my writing studio—grounds me in the world, allowing me to enter abstract terrain via a concrete image, as Green's poem does so deftly.

These days, instead of being on wheel watch on a ship, I step out the front door of my cabin and walk ten steps to my writing studio. Like a fishing boat, my studio is small, with places for everything I need: books, a desk, a rocking chair. I take my seat at the desk, which looks out on a tangle of bamboo and salal, and begin by writing about whatever I see outside the small-paned wood windows. Sometimes my morning poems take the form of haiku, which I can write quickly, wanting to be with whatever is in this moment. At other times, I write notes that, if I'm lucky, gather enough momentum to take flight in a full-fledged poem. Here's a "small noticing" from my journal that could become a poem:

> Last night, rain. This morning,
> I watch a sparrow hop
> across the wet wood deck,
> dip his beak down to sip
> from each nail hole,
> each perfect well
> of imperfection.

When we can begin each day by being fully in the world, noticing even the movements of the sparrow, we bring more of ourselves to the page and more, I hope, to our lives. Perhaps we can begin by considering that everything we see—even the smallest detail—is worthy of our closest attention, our witnessing. We can bring this focused attention and sacred reverence to all that we meet each day. And then we can write it down.

Contemplation Practices

1. Are you able to create a space for yourself that is sanctified in some way? This consecration doesn't have to be much: a small table with some significant objects on it, a candle, a picture, anything that allows you to feel that the time you spend here is different in some way. It might just mean that there's no Internet connection or email accessible in this particular corner.

2. Make it your practice to stop for a few moments in the midst of your morning routine. This could mean breathing in and out three times as you wait for your coffee to brew. It could mean stopping for ten seconds before taking your first bite of breakfast. It could mean driving to work without the radio on, and breathing in and out at stoplights rather than planning the day ahead. See if this small practice changes anything in your mood, your perspective, or your ability to find time for writing.

Writing Practices

1. As Sam Green does in his "Daily Practice" poem from *The Grace of Necessity*, take ten minutes to describe what's right in front of you, wherever you are writing. Keep writing for the whole time, not worrying about the content or the quality. Don't even read this work when you are done. Just shut the notebook and begin your day. These are the "small noticings" that can lead to larger things. After a few weeks, go back and read what you've written to see what kernels you can take away, and what themes or images keep popping up on their own.

2. Try beginning your writing session with a letter to a friend. Something shifts when we feel ourselves not as solitary beings, existing in our solitary ways, but in communion with another. The word *correspondent* means to "co-respond." You and your friend are responding together to the world. In this age of quick, instantaneous, and constant communication, writing a letter can be a welcome break from that quick pace.

   In your letter, start exactly where you are, describing the setting (what you see, smell, hear, touch), and then allow these details to lead you wherever they might go. The poet and essayist Judith Kitchen says of letter writing that "we willingly peel back our defenses to reveal that interior we name the *self*." Allow yourself to write without inhibition, revealing your truest self.

Two

Details, Details, Details

The true secret of happiness lies in the taking a
genuine interest in all the details of daily life.
—William Morris, "The Aims of Art"

Brenda

Once we learn how to slow down, we naturally begin to notice more vividly
what lies right in front of us for our leisurely observation. For example, I live
down the street from an elementary school and a large park filled with old-
growth evergreens, so most mornings I see packs of children walking to school.
When I have the time, I love to sit on my front porch and just be on "wheel
watch," as Holly put it, in my own neighborhood: seeing what I can see.

I see the older kids with their backpacks, girls talking in clumps (always one
girl struggling to keep up, nudged just a little aside from the main group, an
eager tilt to her head—that would have been me at her age). I see boys on
their scooters, yelling to one another, and then the younger kids, kindergartners,
holding the hands of parents, who often have a dog on a leash.

A few minutes later, I'll see the parents and dogs and baby strollers going in the
opposite direction, toward home, their strides now quicker, more purposeful, and
I think about how everyone's day will now unfold—the children safely in school,

learning what they need to know; the dogs back home, in their beds, chewing on rawhide bones; the parents at work or at home, doing what they need to do. All of them sustained by routine. And me here, on the porch, simply bearing witness.

Now here's a latecomer: A mother hugs her son at the corner, yells, "Have a good day" as he walks alone down the sidewalk, too big now to be walked all the way to the schoolroom door, so they've reached this compromise—part way. Part way he can be accompanied; part way, he must travel alone.

All these people and animals walk through the city rose garden next to my house. Every other day, a woman comes to the garden and prunes the dead blooms; she's careful in her work, moving from bush to bush in her straw hat, clipping only those roses that need to be clipped at this exact moment. The remaining flowers gleam from her attention, intensify in color, though she has not touched them at all. She has removed only what gets in the way.

Watching her makes me eager to write. Not to write about anything momentous, but only about the small daily observations that make up our lives. To write about, for instance, the big yellow school bus roaring by, and the children's small heads inside, some of them just barely reaching the windowsills. Noticing this small detail allows me to remember my own walks to school, and how I both yearned for and feared the bus, how I was almost always alone but longed for the company the bus seemed to contain. And then I remember my own eagerness to simply *be* at school, at my wooden desk, where learning seemed almost magical—letters and numbers arranging themselves into miraculous sense. We were told constantly to *pay attention*, and I did, yes, I did.

Now the school bell rings and all the children settle in for the day, listening to their teachers, sharpened pencils scratching against lined paper. I feel as though all morning I've been sharpening my own pencils, preparing myself to write, simply by watching and listening. It's from this kind of observation that I gather both my material for writing and the necessary state of mind, the patience, to sit down and do it.

William Stafford, a poet who often attended to the details of everyday life, describes how these small observations can be a kind of "thread you follow" in order to make meaning of our lives. Here is his poem called "The Way It Is":

> There's a thread you follow. It goes among
> things that change. But it doesn't change.
> People wonder what you are pursuing.
> You have to explain about the thread.
> But it is hard for others to see.
> While you hold it, you can't get lost.
> Tragedies happen; people get hurt
> or die; and you suffer and get old.
> Nothing you do can stop time's unfolding.
> You don't ever let go of the thread.

The poet Robert Bly explains Stafford's metaphor of the thread further. He writes, "Whenever you set a detail down in language, it becomes the end of a thread . . . and every detail—the sound of a lawn mower, the memory of your father's hands, a crack you once heard in lake ice, the jogger hurtling herself past your window—will lead you to amazing riches."

The simplest observations can often lead us to simple wisdom. In her book *On the Threshold: Home, Hardwood, & Holiness,* Elizabeth Jarrett Andrew describes what she observes when entering her house through the back door:

Coming in from the yard, I face shelves overcome with jars: oregano, paprika, and curry roosting in vast extended families; beans, rice, lentils, and bulgur paling in the sunlight; the baking clan (unsweetened chocolate, a jug of honey, coconut, lugubrious molasses, crocks of sugar and flour) awaiting the release of their internal chemistry. Here is the bin for garlic, onions, and potatoes, sprouting their primal appendages. Here are cans of tomatoes and mandarin oranges and coconut milk. Here are the boxes (bright red) of macaroni and cheese. Outside, the garden is wending its weedy way toward zucchini heaven, while inside the ingredients sit, prepared to receive their summons. They will become whatever we make of them.

This amusing inventory—chock-full of detail but also infused with Andrew's humor and perspective—sets her on the way to a deeper meditation on her life, her spiritual path, and her struggle with doubt:

For years I've floundered as my former understandings of God (parental, omnipotent, theistic, held pedestal high) have gone out with the compost, and I'm left mucking around in the dirt looking for holiness. I no longer know what is sacred, what is not, and how to relate to it all. How does one worship the pervasive pulse of life, the seasons' spinning, the pantry's potential? Prayer has been turned inside out, so the words I used to send toward heaven now might as well be spoken to my own mysterious heartbeat, and the guidance that used to come clearly has receded into an indiscernible but beneficent hum. . . .

So I dig down into the details I *do* know: these jumbled jars, these bags of trash. . . . My collection of dry goods doesn't evidence any culinary skills so much as a love for translucent grains of rice, brittle strands of spaghetti, and the shriveled red hides of sun-dried tomatoes within glass jars. The hard beans, black and navy and pinto, feed me with their beautiful waiting bodies long before I pour them into the pot. Abundance greets me each time I enter the house, and I respond with reverence.

After these careful observations of the ordinary details of her home—observations that lead to what seems like an effortless insight—Andrew says: "Anything at all can become the stuff of a spiritual life." That's the lesson we can learn by watching, listening, and being in the world with our full attention. If we train ourselves to be alert, we, too, will experience an abundance that spurs us to "respond with reverence" in our writing.

Holly

Sometimes we need to get away to remember how to pay attention. Some summers I spend a week on Hornby Island in British Columbia at the Grassy Point Guesthouse, where my friends and I eat dinner each evening on a wood deck overlooking the Straits of Georgia, watch the procession of cruise ships heading north, and reminisce about our Alaskan adventures together in summers past. We love to return to this sandstone beach, the open mouths of the tide pools, the orange-billed oystercatchers that greet us on our morning walks. In the morning, we watch a symphony of purple sea stars creep across the tide pools, each leg moving to a tune we can't hear, so slowly we can see their movement only when we, at last, stop moving.

That's the lesson, isn't it? At the community college where I teach English, I team up with a biology colleague to teach a natural history class. I remind our students that they need to pay attention, but how quickly I forget exactly what that means. On the island, to pay attention, I need to get down on my hands and knees and peer into the clear mouths of the tide pools. Only then do I see how one sea star, the color of a pumpkin, slowly extends one of its five legs, clamps it down hard on the sandstone, then does the same with its next leg. Only then do I look more closely at the jigsaw puzzle of orange and purple legs, and notice that another sea star has, in fact, six legs.

One morning I walked the beach with my friend Katy and her ten-year-old son, Lee. While Katy and I study the sea stars, Lee's busy catching baby sculpin with his bare hands. He turns to me and calls out, "Look, Holly, here's another one. This one's really big. Come take a picture of it." Seeing him up to his elbows in the sea reminds me that this curiosity is second nature when we're ten—but we outgrow it. If only we could return to our ten-year-old selves, get down on our hands and knees, and see what details might reward us for our time and close attention.

When we return to the guesthouse, we look up the starfish in the field guide. Lee reads that when starfish lose a leg, they can re-grow it, sometimes even growing a spare. I photographed other exotic creatures in the tide pools to look up, too, so we can begin attaching names to the anemones and sea cucumbers—not just for Lee, but for us. This familiarity—being on a first-name basis with our fellow creatures—is a sign of respect and another aspect of paying attention.

In fact, consider how names and a few scientific details add interest and authority to this excerpt from a poem called "Entering the Kingdom of Invertebrates" by Lee Gulyas, which begins at the edge of a tide pool just like the one we'd observed:

> At the edge of rocky shores
> aggregate anemones cluster by hundreds in pools,
>
> pale green carnivores with pink-tipped tentacles
> clones, elongated, dividing at will
>
> while on the rock above, thousands of barnacles,
> small volcanoes, extend their feathery plumes
>
> and filter food from water. Hermaphrodites,
> they slip their lengthy organs

into any neighbor, a web
of mantle and chamber, simultaneous sexual flurry. . . .

Sea cucumbers and urchins broadcast spawn,

scatter egg and sperm outward, sometimes
floating miles away, into the sea, everything

left to chance. Sometimes it's just that easy.
Medusas drift in currents, transparent, free.

Notice how Gulyas's observations are made more precise by her knowledge of science, not just the names of the creatures, but their sexual habits too, how the "hermaphrodites / . . . slip their lengthy organs / into any neighbor," how it's all "left to chance," and how that intimate knowledge lends the poem both meaning and momentum as the poet ends on the lines: "Sometimes it's just that easy. / Medusas drift in currents, transparent, free."

On the island, whether it's observing the sexual life of jellyfish or letting our thoughts drift with the billowing cumulus clouds, the conditions seem to call us to return to the life of the imagination. As I walk back up the beach, photographing what I see along the way, I begin to inhabit another world altogether, a world that ranges freely in time. Every detail seems significant, prescient: the way the mussel shells lie open to the sea, a spiral shell that seems to point the way. As David James Duncan put it in *River Teeth*: "I suddenly fell through a floor inside myself and landed amid an intensely recollected experience."

Just now, I've dropped into a memory of walking along the lake with Heide, my best friend in high school. It's fall, and we've just come upon, inexplicably, seven perfect red apples washed up on the sand. I'm filled again with our seventeen-year-old sense of wonder, of living in a universe in which apples are offered so freely, so mysteriously. I'm reminded of a book I loved growing up—Anne Morrow Lindbergh's *Gift from the Sea*. When I get back to the guesthouse, I'll take it down from the shelf and read again my favorite passage: "Patience, patience, patience, is what the sea teaches. Patience and faith. One should lie empty, open, choiceless as a beach—waiting for a gift from the sea."

Through writing, reading, and ordinary contemplative practice, we can lie empty and open to any gifts that might wash up wherever we are—not just by the sea or on an island, but wherever we find ourselves—open to all the details that might present themselves for our contemplation.

––––––––––––––––––

Contemplation Practices

1. Spend an hour (or even just a few minutes) on your front porch, front steps, or a park bench, doing nothing. No reading. No writing. Just observing. What do you see? What do you learn about your neighborhood? Also observe your own feelings as you do this exercise: Is it difficult to sit still without distracting yourself? What kinds of thoughts or chatter enter your mind? How do you handle your own resistance to doing nothing? Is there a moment when you can feel your resistance lessening? What does that feel like?

2. Each day, try to look closely at something you think you already know well. This could be a natural object (something in your own garden or a city park) or something man-made (a treasured cup, a knickknack on your shelf). Observe it for longer than a few seconds. Can you pick up on any forgotten or unexpected details?

Writing Practices

1. Write down the sensory details that stay with you from an hour of observation. What did you hear? What did you smell? What did you see? For example, in her poem "Salt Heart," Jane Hirshfield records the sensory details of an afternoon dozing in her backyard—hearing the buzz of a bee in the lavender, the neighbor's trowel hitting stones in the dirt—and in this trance state the poem transforms into a meditation on the transient nature of joy. Here are the beginning lines:

> I was tired,
> half sleeping in the sun.
> A single bee
> delved the lavender nearby,
> and beyond the fence,
> a trowel's shoulder knocked a white stone.
> Soon, the ringing stopped.
> And from somewhere,
> a quiet voice said the one word.
> Surely a command,
> though it seemed more a question,
> a wondering perhaps—"What about joy?"

Notice how she hears what's on the surface, and then allows these details to transcend the physical world. But you don't need to force such meaning. Your observational writings may simply remain "practice" writings that help you hone your powers of observation and description. The most important thing you can learn as a writer is that *all* writing is practice. We have to love the practice itself, and not necessarily the product of that practice.

2. Write a memory of being in school as a young child. What small moment remains lodged in your memory? What got you excited about learning? Can you remember that time, when you were so open to the world? Infuse this memory with sensory details—sights, sounds, smells, tastes, touch—whether or not you think you are making them up. See if these details lead to unexpected insights.

3. As Elizabeth Jarrett Andrew does in *On the Threshold*, write an inventory of everything you see when you enter your home through the door you use most often. What do these things say about you, your life, or your deepest yearnings?

4. To add texture to an observational piece, research the precise names for what you observe as well as interesting facts that might deepen your observations and inform your writing, as Lee Gulyas did in "Entering the Kingdom of Invertebrates."

5. While visiting a beach, forest, or city park—it doesn't need to be wilderness—choose one natural object to observe closely. Sketch it quickly in your notebook as a way of moving into closer connection with it. Once you've done that, brainstorm a list of sensory details to describe it, showing it as vividly and concretely as possible. Then, "go inside" the object, imagining its life from the inside. For example, in his poem "Stone," Charles Simic goes "inside a stone," imagining how it's "cool and quiet" even amid the troubles the stone must endure, even when "a cow steps on it full weight." Like Simic, let your imagination go and see where it takes you.

Three

Lectio Divina

A great poem can open a door in us we may never have known was there. We, as the reader, hold the key to that door. The key is our capacity to listen, to pay attention.

—Roger Housden, *Ten Poems to Change Your Life*

Brenda

For me, a certain kind of poetry or prose—the kind that relies on a patient, observing eye—points out aspects of the world we would never note on our own, and allows me to enter a quieter, more observant state of mind. Sometimes, though, I find it difficult to slow down enough to really read poetry or prose this way, to attend to it as a "reading meditation." In the monastic tradition, it's called *lectio divina*: reading as a sacred act of attention. (See the exercises at the end of this chapter for a fuller description of this practice.) I find I can't really be a writer, or at least the writer I want to be, without being a reader, and I can't be a good reader without creating space for what we might call "contemplative reading." This type of reading becomes a way to be settled and quiet—but also actively alert and awake.

As kids we read this way naturally, completely absorbed in a story, fully focused to the exclusion of every distraction. When I was young, I read this way all the time, and I was always happiest reading, I think now, not just because I enjoyed the narrative but because I felt centered and relaxed—free of the anxiety that plagued me during most of my childhood.

My favorite book was *Charlotte's Web.* I read it over and over, sometimes starting the first page again immediately after finishing the last. Of course, I didn't realize at the time that E. B. White, as an essayist, would also be one of my favorite writers in later years. This same sense of intimacy permeated the essays I also read over and over, trying to learn how to be both so vulnerable and so strong on the page.

Recently I read *Charlotte's Web* again—the same battered copy that has somehow stayed with me all these years, with its soft corners and torn cover—to try to discern how and why this book affected me so. And I saw that this story is really, for me, a Buddhist tale, a lesson in mindfulness. It's about being truly content with whatever and wherever you are. It's a narrative of kindness and compassion. Consider this passage that comes at the very end, after Charlotte has died (yes, I cried again!):

Life in the barn was very good—night and day, winter and summer, spring and fall, dull days and bright days. It was the best place to be, thought Wilbur, this warm delicious cellar, with the garrulous geese, the changing seasons, the heat of the sun, the passage of swallows, the nearness of rats, the sameness of sheep, the love of spiders, the smell of manure, and the glory of everything.

I love that passage, especially Wilbur's almost Zen-like perception that the barn was the "best place to be," no matter what the season. He is aware of all the creatures that share this space with him, the way they abide together in the "glory of everything."

The moral, for me, emerges in the last lines of the book: "It is not often that someone comes along who is a true friend and a good writer. Charlotte was both." I think now that perhaps I've spent my whole life trying to live up to this message: Be a true friend and a good writer. Not a bad way to spend the rest of one's life.

I think about *Charlotte's Web* and my child self curled in bed, nose to nose with the words that would become like scripture for me. Reading was holy back then, and I'd like to remember that state of mind. Perhaps we can always bring a little blessedness into our reading, our writing, and our friendships. *A true friend. A good writer.* Could it really be so hard? Maybe all it takes is a few moments of attention.

Holly

As a kid growing up in the Mississippi River valley, I spent my summers roaming the green hills with my dog, then returning to my room to read. On warm summer evenings, I used to climb out my bedroom window to perch high in the old maple tree with my book, losing track of time as the pages turned as if by the wind, losing myself in words and green leafy silences. Here, while immersed in the words of others, I began to hear the first faint whisper of my own "still, small voice."

I was addicted to reading and loved all its rituals, especially the weekly trip to the downtown library with its smooth marble pillars. I remember vividly the day I got my pink library card and was trusted to take home ten books. Then the difficulty of choosing which ten, and then the next hard choice: which one to read first? I read all the time: at night under the covers with a flashlight, at the breakfast table, in a chair with my cat curled up on my lap. I read aloud to my dog, Simone, or my cat, Mei Ling. I read quickly in those days, devouring books in great chunks despite my mother's admonition to savor them.

Once I had my bicycle and could get to the library on my own, I blissfully ignored her advice. It was a short ride across town, but in these books, I ranged far around the world. I swam in the crystalline blue waters off the California coast in *The Island of the Blue Dolphins*. I drove sled dogs in the frigid Yukon in *The Call of the Wild*. I climbed to the top of the mast in *Treasure Island*. These books allowed me the life of wild adventure I craved, beyond the shady, elm-lined Midwestern streets, the straight rows of corn in the fields.

In college, I learned to read slowly, discovering the pleasure of reading poetry, how each word begged to be spoken aloud and savored for its sounds as well as its meaning. I spent fall afternoons walking the streets of Northfield, Minnesota, kicking dried maple leaves, memorizing my favorite poems by William Butler Yeats and Gerard Manley Hopkins. Many years later, I can still recite most of the lines from Hopkins's "Pied Beauty":

> Glory be to God for dappled things—
>   For skies of couple-colour as a brinded cow;
>   For rose-moles all in stipple upon trout that swim;
> Fresh-firecoal chestnut-falls; finches' wings;
>   Landscape plotted and pieced—fold, fallow, and plough;
>   And all trades, their gear and tackle and trim.
>
> All things counter, original, spare, strange;
>   Whatever is fickle, freckled (who knows how?)
>   With swift, slow; sweet, sour; adazzle, dim;
> He fathers-forth whose beauty is past change:
>   Praise him.

Just try to read this poem without saying it aloud—the rich music of the poem demands to be spoken, the alliteration rolling off our tongues and, like lectio divina, taken into our bodies.

Once you have the reading habit, you never lose it. Even in the last years of her life, while suffering from Alzheimer's disease, my mother still insisted on carrying a book everywhere with her, though she could no longer read. I frequently read to her, that small pleasure one of the few things we could still share.

Now, I read my favorite poems aloud to my friend and former journalism professor, Wilmott Ragsdale (called "Rags" by all his friends), whose eyesight is fading, though his mind—and desire to read—is strong as ever. I'm not sure who enjoys this ritual more. When we sit together in front of the fire, I'm reminded why lectio divina is a sacred act. Words are sustenance, as essential to our spirits as food to our bodies. This is why we fall in love with certain poets and their poetry: because they invite us to slow down, to savor the taste of each word and then, to begin to listen for our own quiet voices.

Contemplation Practices

1. Choose a small passage from a book you love. Practice lectio divina, reading slowly, seeing how each word or phrase strikes you and moves you on to the next. Read it aloud. Really get into it.

2. Do the same thing with a group of people, reading the passage aloud. Discuss which lines, images, or words resonated with you.

3. Go back to a childhood book that was important to you. Re-read it (you can try this as a practice of lectio divina), seeing if a particular passage stands

About Lectio Divina

As described by poet and teacher Mary Rose O'Reilley in *The Garden at Night*, in *lectio divina* monks read the scripture as though "feasting on the word." This means to read the text line by line, first "taking a bite (*Lectio*), then chewing on it (*Meditatio*). Next is the opportunity to savor the essence of it (*Oratio*). Finally, the Word is digested and made a part of the body (*Contemplatio*)."

This method is all about listening: reading as a way to listen more acutely. But lectio does not have to be reserved for the religious; it can be a purely secular activity. O'Reilley writes: "When I'm teaching literature, we often practice lectio divina, which involves reading very small snatches of text, stopping, and pondering, as though each poem were a sacred text." As she describes it, here is the process of lectio:

~ First, "center yourself in body, mind, and purpose."

~ Read a selected passage or poem slowly, several times, while simply noticing what is happening in each line. Reading aloud helps you slow down and pause at any phrase, image, or word that resonates for you. Noticing means you don't judge or interpret or analyze—you simply notice. This is "taking the bite."

~ Consider: What speaks to you in this piece? What images lodge in you? Why?

~ Finally, you can enter into a dialogue with this passage, allowing your own memories, images, or words to come forth in response.

out to you now. Sit with that passage and see what it has to tell you as an adult. What kind of life lesson now seems embedded in those pages?

4. Choose a poem that begs to be read aloud and commit it to memory. If the poem is written in meter, try reciting it while walking, allowing the cadence of your steps to emphasize the meter, yet another way of feeling the poem in your body.

Writing Practices

1. Write a reply to your lectio reading. Either articulate your understanding of this passage in a new way or write your own scene, image, or story in response.

2. Take a random line from the piece you read as lectio and put it as the first line or the title of your own poem or prose piece. Write from this image or idea, allowing each new image or detail to be triggered by the one before it. Try to write nonstop for ten minutes. Try to turn off your editorial mind and simply be open to whatever words come your way. This exercise can be especially fun to do with others, seeing what different pieces you create from the same trigger. It can be a standard warm-up exercise you do every day, as it gives you a place to start.

3. Write a scene of yourself reading your favorite book (or being read to) as a child. Why did you love this book? Why did you love reading? Choose one specific moment and try to suspend it in time. Where did you like to read? Describe this place as specifically as possible. Capture all the sensory details.

What sounds or smells accompany you? Can you convey this as a contemplative or holy moment?

4. Write a scene of yourself in a library as a child. Capture the sensory details and see if any unexpected details arise to show you new things about the history of yourself as a reader.

5. Write a scene in which you observe a friend, family member, or other loved one reading a book. What is he or she reading? What is the body's posture, the expression on the face? What do you hear in the place where reading is happening? What is going on around the reader and how does the act of reading create stillness within that activity? What can you learn about this person through this particular scene?

Four

Opening the Senses

To begin to understand the gorgeous fever that is consciousness,
we must try to understand the senses and what they can tell us
about the ravishing world we have the privilege to inhabit.

—Diane Ackerman, *A Natural History of the Senses*

Brenda

I once spent a weekend at the North Cascades Institute, where my friends and I wrote, paddled canoes, and sat on the deck with the chef peeling garlic, talking about mindfulness in our food choices. Though we spent only forty-eight hours there, those hours expanded in ways that can seem so elusive in ordinary life. It seems that when we are fully awake, slowing down and really taking in the world with all our senses, time becomes more flexible, more primal, and a day (even a minute) can hold much more than we ever thought possible.

One afternoon I took a walk up a forested trail with my friend Katie, who has been trained to work with the deaf and the blind. She blindfolded me and placed my hand firmly on her elbow to guide me along the path. It was an eerie sensation; immediately I became intensely mindful of the texture of the path, of the way my feet touched the ground. I felt like I was experiencing myself from the inside out, my entire body an antenna, picking up signals I had never noticed before. My ears seemed to amplify every sound: the rustle of a bird in the brush, the call of a voice far away across the lake, my own footfalls on the path. I smelled mushrooms in the soil, crushed leaves, Katie's shampoo. Katie's arm provided a stable guide, and I was able to simply follow, to feel my body situated in space in all three dimensions.

We can also do this without the blindfold, if we're aware of the need to hone our senses in order to both fully experience and translate the world. In one of my favorite passages from Joan Didion's essay "Goodbye to All That," she calls up the sights and sounds and tastes and scents and even the tactile *feel* of Manhattan to help her reader really experience what it was like to be a young girl on the verge of adulthood, on her own in this exciting new city:

> That first night I opened my window on the bus into town and watched for the skyline, but all I could see were the wastes of Queens and the big signs that said midtown tunnel this lane and then a flood of summer rain. . . . And for the next three days I sat wrapped in blankets in a hotel room air conditioned to 35 degrees and tried to get over a bad cold and a high fever. It did not occur to me to call a doctor, because I knew none, and although it did occur to me to call the desk and ask that the air conditioner be turned off, I never called, because I did not know how much to tip whoever might come—was anyone ever so young? I am here to tell you that someone was.

Didion's long sentences emphasize the way all these images are coming at the narrator as she breathlessly takes it all in. She reaches out to the reader—"was anyone ever so young? I am here to tell you that someone was"—an endearing acknowledgement of her own innocence. Later, we walk with her through the city, experiencing the streets with her, all our senses on high alert:

I remember walking across Sixty-second Street one twilight that first spring, or the second spring, they were all alike for a while. I was late to meet someone but I stopped at Lexington Avenue and bought a peach and stood on the corner eating it and . . . I could taste the peach and feel the soft air blowing from a subway grating on my legs and I could smell lilac and garbage and expensive perfume and I knew that it would cost something sooner or later.

Can't you just feel it, the way the world has spiraled to a standstill at that moment, in the midst of a busy sidewalk? The taste of the peach mingles with smell of lilac and the feel of the air blowing up from underground. Everything is granted the full measure of her attention—the smell of garbage no less important than the smell of expensive perfume.

As I age, I sometimes feel my senses dulling, but it doesn't take much to reawaken the senses, to really breathe in the smell of your coffee in the morning, the bright tang of orange peel, or to really hear the noise in the streets not as a distraction but as a soundtrack full of nuance. And then, there you are, thick in the middle of your life, with all the time in the world.

Holly

All our senses are important—for both living and writing—but as we've evolved, we've had less practical need for our sense of smell; now it's likely our most over-looked sense. But for many creatures, smell is essential to survival. According to scientists, salmon find their way back from a four-thousand-mile journey across the ocean by sniffing their way down the rocky coast until they find the stream of their birth. Dogs dispense with polite greetings and instead check each other out by sniff-ing. Ask anyone who's spent time with a dog: It's not sight but smells that matter.

My dog, Fox, sets out on his daily walk each morning, tail wagging, eager to see what new scents the day might bring. His nose is unerring: He can sniff out the scent of a cat that passed through five minutes ago, an otter that scrambled over the rocks on the beach hours earlier, a French fry tossed out someone's car window days ago.

As I watch him track smells, nose hovering an inch above the ground, I can't help but wonder what we've lost, living in our world of sights and sounds. What closed rooms in our own lives could be opened if our noses were still as attuned to smell as Fox's? I recently read that a dog's sense of smell is believed to be a thousand times more sensitive than that of humans, with forty-four times the number of sensory receptors. Imagine the rich smorgasbord of scent we walk past each day, unaware.

I've also read that smell, our most primitive sense, is both the first sense we are aware of—the smell of our mother's breast—and the last sense we lose. I know in my own life how inextricably linked it is to memory, how a whiff of damp concrete will conjure up my grandmother's basement with its worn wooden railings and uneven steps, moisture weeping from the concrete walls, but beyond the stairs, shelf upon shelf of canned peaches, pears, and beans, lined up like jewels. Or how the smell of Pine Sol still conjures up memories of the damp cinderblock bathhouse at the camp in northern Minnesota where I spent my summers. And more recently, how, when I came across a blue flannel shirt that had been my mother's and that still held her distinctive scent, a whiff of it still brought unexpected tears to my eyes ten years after her death.

Many good poems illustrate why it's important to appeal to all the reader's senses, but here's one part of a classic poem by T. S. Eliot, "Preludes," that creates an evocative scene using several senses in just a few lines:

The winter evening settles down
With smell of steaks in passageways.
Six o'clock.
The burnt-out ends of smoky days.
And now a gusty shower wraps
The grimy scraps
Of withered leaves about your feet
And newspapers from vacant lots;
The showers beat
On broken blinds and chimney-pots,
And at the corner of the street
A lonely cab-horse steams and stamps.
And then the lighting of the lamps.

While all the images are vivid, note how much is added by the two lines that evoke smells, specifically: "with smell of steaks in passageways" and "the burnt-out ends of smoky days." Suddenly, we find ourselves standing beside the poet, smelling the smoke- and steak-drenched air, transported to a lonely street in London on a bleak winter night.

Now, when I return from our walk to sit at my desk, I try to bring Fox's enthusiasm for all he encounters, such as his delight in the taste of the tall blades of green grass he eats as we head back up the hill. Isn't this how we all want to be in the world? We need to remember that we, too, are animals; we must trust our animal senses, which once we depended on to stay alive. Think if we had the visual acuity of the peregrine falcon, which can spot a field mouse in the grass from seventy feet in the air. Or think if we still responded as instinctually as that field mouse, sensing that shadow looming high above us. We've all seen how other birds scatter when a hawk or eagle glides onto the scene. Imagine being that closely tied to all our senses and to our own survival, that fully alive in our own bodies.

As writers, we're invited to call up the heightened senses of our lost animal nature. When we walk, we can be alert to—and delight in—those stray whiffs of cottonwood, mock orange, lemon verbena as we pass our neighbor's garden, then let those smells transport us where they will: the adored aunt whose towels always smelled of lemon verbena, muggy summers swatting mosquitoes beneath the cottonwood. As writers, we're invited to live in all our senses, then carry that awareness to the page so our readers can dwell there too.

Contemplation Practices

1. Try a "blindfold" experiment with a friend. In a safe place, move through the world with one of your senses diminished to see how the other senses might yield different experiences.

2. Observe your pet or an animal in the park or a zoo. In what ways are this animal's senses heightened? Try to imagine for a few minutes what it would be like to live with an animal's sense of perception.

Writing Practices

1. Has there been a moment in your life when time seemed to stop or expand? Describe that scene in writing, really suspending the moment in time. How much can a moment hold? As Joan Didion did in "Goodbye to All That" or T. S. Eliot in "Preludes," consciously include sensory details, trying to hit on every sense. You might be surprised at what you can remember.

2. Write about smells from your childhood—list five smells you remember well, then choose one to explore more. What associations do you have with that smell? Is there an emotional memory that goes along with it? Write about that memory.

3. Write an early childhood memory, seeking to incorporate all of the senses, even those you normally don't use, even if you think you're making it up. What are the sounds in the background? What do you smell? What do you touch and how does it feel? What taste is in your mouth? By doing this exercise, you're training yourself to pay attention to the senses as a way of translating memory into concrete details.

4. Write a description of a memorable incident without drawing on the sense of sight. See what other senses you can call upon to evoke the scene.

Five

Preparation Is Everything

Fortune favors the prepared mind.
—Louis Pasteur

Brenda

As a young writer, I don't think I really understood that you need to *prepare* for writing; I figured you could just sit down and begin. But I've come to see that I need to be warmed up. I need to have something gestating in my head, even if it's just a little niggling idea, unformed and unknowable until I start to lure it out.

Oddly enough, the radio is one of my greatest sources of preparation for writing. I'm a devoted public radio fan, and ever since I discovered podcasts I'm able to listen to my favorite shows—*The Splendid Table, To the Best of Our Knowledge, This American Life, Radiolab*—any time I want. I put them on while I'm cooking, while I'm cleaning, while I'm doing yoga in the morning. The familiar voice of Lynn Rossetto Kasper can be enough to shake me out of a bad mood. The theme music for *To the Best of Our Knowledge* automatically makes me alert, because I know I'm about to hear something that will blow my mind. And so much fodder for my work comes from little snippets that stick in my brain while the radio murmurs on in the background; these images, facts and stories gestate in my mind, and then emerge once I sit down to write. So even though I *look* like I'm just half-listening to the radio while I do my morning routines, I'm actually preparing to write.

In her book *The Creative Habit*, choreographer Twyla Tharp emphasizes that the ritual of preparation can be even more paramount than the act of creativity itself. Her own form of preparation goes like this:

> I begin each day of my life with a ritual: I wake up at 5:30 a.m., put on my workout clothes, my leg warmers, my sweatshirts, and my hat. I walk outside my Manhattan home, hail a taxi, and tell the driver to take me to the Pumping Iron gym at 91st Street and First Avenue, where I work out for two hours. The ritual is not the stretching and weight training I put my body through each morning at the gym; the ritual is the cab. The moment I tell the driver where to go I have completed the ritual.

Tharp goes on to tell stories of other artists and their rituals: Stravinsky started each day by sitting down at the piano to play a Bach fugue; a chef she knows starts his day by puttering among his plants in his terrace garden. Flaubert was rumored to sniff a drawer of apples; another writer painstakingly sharpened a row of pencils. The rituals one uses can be anything, large or small, that puts you in a creative frame of mind. Tharp's ritual is hailing the cab, a small gesture that signals to her body and her brain that she's *ready.*

Tharp also talks about what she calls "scratching": the seemingly unimportant things we do so that ideas will take root. We can "scratch" anywhere; scratching can be reading, eavesdropping, going to an art exhibit, looking at the tabloids or, yes, listening to the radio. "Reading, conversation, environment, culture, heroes, mentors, nature," Tharp writes, "all are lottery tickets for creativity. Scratch away at them, and you'll find out how big a prize you've won."

Whether we're preparing for writing or "scratching" for ideas, we don't really know what will happen. We have to do the small tasks so that the big work will emerge on its own terms. All of it is preparation for the work—*and* it's the work itself.

Holly

I've been thinking about preparedness, and what it means as my partner, John, and I get ready for a week of what's predicted to be record-setting cold temperatures, snow, and maybe even a wind storm. I love all the rituals of winter: laying straw down over all the fragile plants, the figs, passion flower, clematis, and the blueberries, too, for good measure. I've unearthed the covers for the faucets, wrapped any exposed pipes, even found the draft dodgers to cover the gap at the base of my cabin's old doors (which I couldn't bear to give up when we remodeled). I do all this because I know it means I can enjoy this stretch of cold weather, not worry I'll lose pipes or plants. I grew up in Minnesota; these are deeply ingrained habits that remind me of home.

I also think about how we need to prepare as writers, clear the decks, court the muse for what small gift of words we might receive. On the radio show *Writer's Almanac*, I learned that the Pulitzer Prize–winning Egyptian writer Naguib Mahfouz took a ninety-minute walk around Cairo every morning, then read a newspaper at a café before sitting down to write. This preparation appears to have served him well—he wrote over fifty novels before he died at ninety-four.

One poem that has served as a touchstone for me captures the importance of preparation for any artist or writer: "The Woodcarver" from *The Way of Chuang-Tzu*, edited and translated by Thomas Merton. In the poem, Khing, a woodcarver, describes how his carving a bell stand could take place only after a week of spiritual preparation:

> I guarded my spirit, did not expend it
> On trifles, that were not to the point.

He fasts for seven days, and after this rigorous spiritual practice, Khing describes how he goes into the forest to select the tree for the bell stand:

> When the right tree appeared before my eyes
> The bell stand also appeared in it, clearly, beyond doubt.
> All I had to do was to put forth my hand
> And begin.

While we may not choose to fast for seven days, we can remind ourselves of the necessity of guarding our spirits so they can do their creative work, how we need to fend off the myriad distractions we confront each day in order to be open to whatever the world presents to us, to be able to see our own bell stand waiting in the tree.

When I was fishing years ago—long before I'd read "The Woodcarver"—I wrote about preparation in a poem for a Yugoslavian fisherman, Marco, who taught me to hang gillnets in his basement. I was eager to get the nets hung for our first season of gillnetting; at twenty-six, I was filled with the impatience of youth but, thankfully, I came to understand that I was to learn this skill on Marco's terms and at his pace. Soon I began to look forward to hearing Marco's slow, measured steps on the old wood stairs as he came down to check my hangings, then invite me up for a lengthy diversion of coffee, doughnuts, and stories in his kitchen. I came to understand that he was teaching me much more than how to hang gillnets.

When I began the poem, I wanted to thank him for teaching me, and when the poem ended—in a different place than I expected, as poems often do—I hoped I'd succeeded. Here's an excerpt from that poem, "Preparation Is Everything":

> Now we climb the old wooden steps for dinner,
> go to the kitchen, where you remind me
> *preparation is everything:*
>
> *Cut the cabbage like this, little slices,*
> *fine, bit by bit it becomes cole slaw*
> *but you gotta have a sharp knife, you hear?*
> *Just a little bit at a time. Like this.*
> *Minnie makes the cole slaw, but I always cut it.*
> *Fine, real fine.*

In the midst of our lives, we can try to remember Marco's reminder that "preparation is everything." We can pause and be willing to do the work *before* the work—like the woodcarver, we can be attentive to what the tree might reveal, or how any mundane task might call for us to approach it, carefully, with reverence.

———————————

Contemplation Practices

1. Use the common, everyday things around you as sources of inspiration. Become a receptive ground for ideas. Write down odd facts or conversations you hear on the radio, on the bus, in line at the store. Think of this as "eavesdropping meditation."

2. Using Twyla Tharp's idea of "scratching," reflect on the activities you do when you have an idea simmering, when you want to make space for it to emerge. Do you pull weeds, putter in the garage, organize the junk drawer, take the dog for a walk?

3. In her book *The Artist's Way*, Julia Cameron suggests making "an artist's date" with yourself as another way to nurture your creativity. Make a list of museums or exhibits in your neighborhood and visit one next time you need a creative jump-start.

Writing Practices

1. In your past, was there something you needed to prepare for on a daily basis? What was your ritual of preparation? Write this down in one detailed scene.

2. Was there some special or extraordinary event you needed to prepare for? (A performance, a wedding, your first day at work, and so on.) What were the small things that led to the big act?

3. Describe a time that you were able to be open to what the world presented, when you could see the "bell stand" waiting for you in the tree. What enabled you to see it? In what ways had you prepared for it?

Six

Practice, Practice, Practice

Every artist must sometimes believe that art is the doorway
to the divine. Perhaps it is. But it's dangerous for a musician to
philosophize instead of practicing.

—Glenn Kurtz, *Practicing*

Brenda

As a kid, I always kind of envied the other children who had something to
practice: violin, piano, basketball, gymnastics. Though most of them claimed
to hate it and slunk into their practices with pouts and glares, they still seemed
to have a sense of purpose about them, carrying their sturdy black instrument
cases, or changing into their uniforms. It's not my parents' fault; I probably
adamantly refused all lessons to the point of hysteria, afraid of failure, and so I
wandered rather aimlessly in my backyard, *pretending* to practice. Like Snoopy,
I became "world famous": the world-famous gymnast practicing her round off
from the jungle gym; the world-famous basketball star, clumsily dribbling my
brother's basketball on the makeshift court. What did I yearn for so much, as I
did my solitary, imaginary practices in the backyard? I think it was the sense of
growing *better* at something—a visible, tangible manifestation of growth.

Now, as an adult, I still don't have a musical instrument or a sport to practice, but I do practice writing. In his book *The Muses among Us: Eloquent Listening and Other Pleasures of the Writer's Craft*, Kim Stafford likens writing to playing the violin. He says that a violin, played every day, will keep the vibrations of the music in its body, even while lying still and silent. If it is not played every day, the vibrations dissipate and the wood grows lifeless. "An instrument dies if not played daily," he writes. "A guitar, a violin, a lute chills the air for the first fifteen minutes of fresh play. . . . But the fiddle played every day hangs resonant on the wall, quietly boisterous when first it is lifted down, already trembling, anxious to speak, to cry out, to sing at the bow's first stroke."

The word *discipline* is an extension of the word *disciple*, and if we consider ourselves disciples of writing, we might find the energy and devotion we need to keep going, even when it feels like the practice is arduous. In his book *Practicing: A Musician's Return to Music*, concert guitarist Glenn Kurtz writes of practice: "Whatever 'music' is for you, if you practice for real, eventually it will show you everything that is within you. Because as accomplished or as disappointed as you may feel now, you don't know what remains concealed in your hands." We can reclaim the word *practice*, as Kurtz has, and see practice itself as the point. We are always practicing, until the very end. And we can do so with patience, without striving, making practice an end in itself.

Sometimes, though, you need to rustle up some allies in this endeavor in order to keep your practice going. Lately I've been doing a writing practice with my friends Nancy and Katie. We often meet in a café, and after about twenty minutes of catch-up time, we pull out our notebooks and get to work. All we're doing is writing sentences, and allowing those sentences to guide us. Using a process that Nancy has taught us, we each scribble random "start lines" on scraps of paper (these can be random lines from books we've brought with us, or simply phrases that have come up in conversation), and then we begin writing from those start lines. In the first segment of five minutes, we write sentences with only a few words. In the next segment of ten minutes, we "chain" sentences together (the last word of one sentence begins the next). In the next session, we write one long sentence for twenty minutes.

The writing segments—timed with a kitchen timer, with the bustle of the world going on around us—are a kind of intense, active meditation; we need to be fiercely in the "now" in order for it to work. If we get distracted by someone at the next table, we write the conversation into the piece. We breathe, and forget to breathe, and let out long sighs, the writing arm growing stronger as the weeks go on, the writing brain stretching its muscles, aiming for flexibility. The writing generated by this intensive focus on form over content paradoxically leads to content we would never have written any other way; it bypasses all the filters in our brains. It's raw, emotional, infused with the energy of the sentence that bears it.

When we finish each timed segment, we read the work aloud to one another, but we don't comment on it, not yet. We simply notice any images that seemed particularly powerful or ripe for further exploration. Later, at home, in our own writing spaces, we can type up what we have in our notebooks, start shaping this raw writing into something that might make sense.

Not everything will make it that far, of course; much of the work is simply practice, warming up. It helps to have friends doing this with me, as I doubt I'd have the patience to practice so hard by myself. It's kind of like being in my yoga class, where the others sweat along with me, breathing hard as we hold a pose longer than we could ever do on our own.

Enlisting a teacher can also help bring your writing to a new level, just as it would in music, visual art, or sports. For example, I once had a private lesson with my yoga teacher, Michal. She lined me up against the wall. "The wall is your friend," she said. "The wall will show you in an instant what it would take me a million words to explain." And she was right. As I did the poses I thought I knew so well, I felt which muscles really had to work, especially a small muscle just above my hip I had never noticed before. "Oh, my," I said. Michal said, "Exactly. We love that muscle. That muscle connects everything."

I didn't love the wall the whole time. At times I wanted to push back against the wall, tell it to just *leave me alone!* I wanted to go back to what I knew I could already do well. Finally I came away from the wall and did the poses again under Michal's watchful eye. My body retained the memory and the poses felt different—more layered, more complex. That little muscle in my back was still alive, singing, guiding everything.

Now I think of writing the same way. Once you reach a certain comfortable level in your writing, it can be tempting to stay there, especially if we receive praise or validation for what we do well. That's fine for a while. But at some point we may want to push ourselves further or find a coach who will guide us to another level.

We need to train deeply, alone and with others to support and guide us. Going on retreats offers this kind of intense training—a writing retreat, a meditation retreat, a nature retreat—or, in this case, all three. Maybe we can have a "private session" with someone—a teacher, a fellow writer, who can point out where we are getting lazy and just doing things in our habitual ways, blind to the next level. Or maybe we spend a day copying out sentences or poems from writers we admire, getting their rhythms into our hands, feeling their wise presence among us. Whatever it is, it will build up our writing stamina, our strength.

Isn't that what we're after, in these practices that open us up to ourselves and each other in profound ways? To feel ourselves stretching. To feel ourselves in the presence of someone or something that *cares*. To feel that little click when everything falls into place.

Holly

I'm at the North Cascades Institute with my friend and meditation teacher Kurt Hoelting to teach a weekend workshop called "Sit, Walk, Write: Nature and the Practice of Presence." We're gathered together in the outdoor amphitheater to meet and welcome the forty-five participants, many of whom have driven many hours and miles to be here. The group is larger than we expected and I confess to feeling apprehensive about how it will work, sharing solitude—and the quiet beauty of this place—with so many people. But I also know the beauty of practicing together, of learning to trust each other in sharing silence, that our individual practice can be enriched and steadied by the sense of solidarity, the presence of the person next to you, breathing together, *in and out*.

As we go around the circle, introducing ourselves, my eyes keep drifting up to the alpenglow on the high peaks behind us. In this place, especially, I feel the presence not just of the other participants but of the writers who've come before us. As I look up at Sourdough Mountain, I can't help but think of Gary Snyder and Philip Whalen, who spent several seasons high up in a fire lookout, Jack Kerouac across the way at Desolation Peak, and all the words written here, the practices these writers did in concert with this beautiful landscape.

I'm reminded that whenever we come together, we bring the presence not just of those who are with us, but of a much larger community: the books that have informed us, and the writers who've nudged us along, helping to shape our views.

By the second day, we've settled into a rhythm of sitting, walking, and writing in silence, both inside our classroom and out in the fall sunlight streaming through the aspens and birches. Though our large circle reaches all four walls of the room, we've found that sitting in silence together makes it all work; what might feel crowded is beginning to feel more and more like rich community as we move back and forth between silence and sharing.

We hike up to the waterfall halfway up Sourdough Mountain, and each of the forty-five participants peels off the path to find his or her own "sit spot," as Adam the naturalist calls it, a place to sit in the silence of the fall woods, reflect, and write. As Adam comes down the path, he calls us all back with a raven call so authentic I peer into the tops of the Douglas firs and aspens, looking for the bird. We return, each from our own small island of leafy silence, to gather again in a circle and read aloud, our words shimmering between us like the last golden leaves of the aspens holding the late summer sun.

At the end of the last day, we all sit quietly in the dining room with tea, looking out over the lake, each with our journals, trying to capture this exquisite day in words, watching it slip away. Earlier, during one of our periods of meditation, I sat on a low, flat rock above the lake at the end of the log boom, noticing how the surface is agitated outside the log boom, serene within. It seems a perfect analogy for the last few days; we've seen how sitting, walking, and writing in silence enables these ripples to smooth out, at least until the next disturbance comes along.

Tonight we'll gather one last time, each with our own disturbances, breathing in and out, following our breath until our minds are as serene as the glimmering blue surface of the lake. Kurt will ring the bell and we'll drop down, slowly, into the shared silence that now feels as comfortable as an old sweatshirt, supporting each other in this practice, holding together and savoring the last golden minutes of this fleeting fall season. If we're lucky, perhaps the spirits of Snyder, Kerouac, and Whalen—and all the writers we admire—will join their words with ours.

Contemplation Practices

1. Reflect on what you practiced as a child. How did you feel about it? Was practice something you dreaded or embraced? What do you practice today? Think about all the skills and habits of mind you practice each day—and how those practices make you who you are.

2. Find a friend or friends to practice sitting quietly together. You may already have your own meditation practice, but it helps to have a *sangha*—a community—even if it's just a *sangha* of two. Set a regular time to practice together each week. It works best if you just set a time and place and all show up—no phone calls or emails—just a time that you agree to set aside each week to sit together.

Writing Practices

1. Try a timed writing practice, alone or with others. You can use technical considerations—like the long sentence—or be more free-form, writing from random topics and start lines. Consider this a kind of "writing meditation," not directing the work too much, allowing yourself to breathe. Natalie Goldberg, in *Writing Down the Bones*, describes simple timed writing practices you can do alone or with others. As you continue to practice this way, you will be able to "hit the ground running" whenever you sit down to write.

2. Write some scenes about something you practiced a lot as a child or a teenager. What was this practice like? Who was your coach or teacher? What kind of discipline did it require? If you stopped practicing this, why did you stop? What do you practice now?

3. Find friends who are willing to hike or walk together in silence, then set aside twenty minutes to find a quiet place to sit alone. Just sit for the first ten minutes: seeing, listening, smelling. Then write for ten minutes about what you have experienced. You can do this in a city park, a shopping mall, or out in the wilderness. Then share your writings with each other.

4. Joan Didion has said that she learned to write by spending a summer copying Hemingway's sentences longhand. Choose a writer you especially admire and copy a few pages from a work to get the rhythms of his or her sentences in your body. Consider this writer your "coach," helping you to develop your writing muscles.

Seven

Contemplation at Work

> It is perhaps not widely enough recognized that most healthy contemplative traditions were designed to be practiced in the midst of noise, because noise is what *is*. For me, contemplation has been not a retreat but a path of tender emergence. . . . The contemplative does not resist the world, but learns to enter it.
>
> —Mary Rose O'Reilley, *The Garden at Night*

Brenda

When I left college, I was trained to be a journalist but never had the drive or guts to really be one. Instead, I wandered up the coast of California, working as a cook for a summer camp, then as a massage therapist at a hot springs resort. All of these jobs I had just kind of "fallen into," with little sense of what I was really doing, but with each job I did feel a kind of immersion in the tasks at hand. As a cook in a busy kitchen swarming with children, I somehow managed to smile and make delicious cauldrons of soup, huge casseroles of lasagna. At the hot springs resort, my work as a massage therapist was deeply satisfying; people came to me already warm and relaxed from the hot baths, and my job was simply to kneel at their sides, lay my hands on them, be as present as possible. Each massage seemed like a dance—not really work, but a giving of myself in a way that felt wholly pleasurable.

As I prepared to leave that place after four years—still young, still just being formed—my friend Rhea gave me a book of Marge Piercy poems. She had bookmarked one in particular, "To Be of Use," and from the very first stanza I knew it could be a kind of guiding light as I left Orr Springs, searching out a new way of being in the world, a vocation:

> The people I love the best
> jump into work head first
> without dallying in the shallows
> and swim off with sure strokes almost out of sight.
> They seem to become natives of that element,
> the black sleek heads of seals
> bouncing like half submerged balls. . . .
>
> I want to be with people who submerge
> in the task, who go into the fields to harvest
> and work in a row and pass the bags along,
> who stand in the line and haul in their places,
> who are not parlor generals and field deserters
> but move in a common rhythm
> when the food must come in or the fire be put out.
>
> The work of the world is common as mud.
> Botched, it smears the hands, crumbles to dust.
> But the thing worth doing well done
> has a shape that satisfies, clean and evident . . .

Now I work as a teacher in a state university, a job that can be stressful and full of petty annoyances, but my best moments come when I shuck off all that distracts me and simply "jump into work head first," without "dallying" in resistance. My best moments come when I can be with my students fully, allowing a class or a conversation to unfold organically, delighting in the surprises that come when they, too, "move in a common rhythm" so that our work can be something pleasurable we do together.

This isn't always the case, of course. Sometimes my work is "botched" and I'm learning—oh so slowly!—to move on, glean what I can from my mistakes, not try to fix everything so that it's perfect. All we have is the work at hand. All we have is the moment right in front of us. And within that moment we have the laundry and the dishes and all the ordinary things of our lives.

Sometimes our most ordinary physical activities can be the ones that lead us to the greatest moments of stillness and epiphany. I'm thinking of Billy Collins's wonderful poem "Shoveling Snow with Buddha," in which the poet turns the mundane chore of clearing his driveway into a contemplative practice ripe with humor and perspective. Here is an excerpt:

> . . . here we are, working our way down the driveway,
> one shovelful at a time.
> We toss the light powder into the clear air.
> We feel the cold mist on our faces.
> And with every heave we disappear
> and become lost to each other
> in these sudden clouds of our own making,
> these fountain-bursts of snow. . . .

He has thrown himself into shoveling snow
as if it were the purpose of existence,
as if the sign of a perfect life were a clear driveway
you could back the car down easily
and drive off into the vanities of the world.

What would it be like, I wonder, if we could do all the work we need to do as if the Buddha were at our side, pitching in? What would it be like to "disappear" into our work, knowing that whatever we are doing right now—whether it be sublime or mundane—truly is "the purpose of existence"? I suspect we'd be a tad bit happier (and probably get a lot more done, to boot).

We really can't separate our "contemplative" lives from our "real" lives. Nor can we separate the writing mind from the working mind—that would drive us crazy. Since work is so much of what we do—work at our jobs, work at home—we need to learn how to bring ourselves wholeheartedly into that work and to consider it rich material for writing.

In the midst of our everyday lives, so many things call out to be handled, both tangible and intangible things. "Fix this, please," is the message that comes through all our portals: on the phone, in emails, in the bank statements sailing through the mail slot, in the cry of a child or a friend. "Fix it," they plead. Or your own mind, mulling over the past or fretting about the future.

It seems that much of our practice—in meditation, in writing, in living—is learning discernment and acceptance. Learning what really needs to be fixed and what can be accepted as it is. And even when we do need to fix something—whether it be a flooded basement or a perilous frame of mind—we can learn how to do so with equanimity rather than distress. And we can look at this moment as an opportunity for writing.

For example, I once wrote a little piece about the dirty windows in my house. It began with simple observation:

The sun is out in Bellingham, Washington, which means that most women I know, including me, are staring at our dirty windows. Not out them, but *at* them. We're seeing the streaks, the smudges, the fingerprints, the coating of dust, the firm outlines of water drops left over from the hard rains of winter. We're looking up the phone number of our window cleaners—that nice couple with the VW bug—or we're considering the time and effort of getting out our own Windex, our rags, our squeegees, and spending this nice day getting our arms sore spritzing, and wiping, and squeaking, and spritzing again.

Or we shift our gaze and see the inches of cat and dog hair in the corners of our wood floors, the fur spread like a second mat on the living room rug. We're seeing the cobwebs dangling from the corners of the ceilings, forming filaments of dirty lace across the tops of our cabinets. We're seeing the age spots on our hands, our unpedicured toes, the hair on our legs coarse and dark after a winter of long pants, leggings, and tights. We're seeing all the things that are normally covered up, or blissfully ignored, for most of our cloudy days in the Northwest—that gray light so silver, so soft, so forgiving.

After really seeing the dirty windows—and how this observation reflects an inner state of mind as well—I allowed myself to muse on *why* I'm noticing these things; I allowed my intuition to keep drawing me forward:

Perhaps that is why most of us feel drawn to live here, in the far north corner of the nation, with our preponderance of muted days; it's why we have migrated back here after brief sojourns in drier and sunnier lands—Southern California, Montana, Utah—places where the sun shines a lot, where the landscapes are certainly beautiful in their dry, vivid ways, but where we never felt truly at home. *No*, we say, *give us cloud cover*. A damp breeze. The smell of moist earth that greets you as you deplane on the tarmac of a tiny airport. Give us indirect light; we are plants that thrive in partial shade.

We sigh at our dirty windows, and we wonder if perhaps we've been aching *inside*, too, for a light that is a little more soft, more forgiving—a light that fusses about us and pulls our garments just so to hide any flaws. When I first started a meditation practice more than thirty years ago, I expected that kind of shimmer, a gentle beam, but instead got the full brunt of direct light through dirty windows, a glare that makes you squint. You see every smudge on your character, every fingerprint on your soul, every trace of rains long gone. I closed my eyes, said my mantra, and wished for a cloudy day, one that might wash me in pearls.

Thus this simple observation of something so mundane—dirty windows—leads me gently to my greater concerns: my yearning for soft forgiveness in all aspects of my life. In this piece, I work from the outside in, because I've trained myself to do so. The short essay goes on to describe my yoga practice, and how it seems to finally provide the respite I seek, for a few minutes a week. The writing became spiritual, even though it started with something as non-spiritual as dirt.

So we don't need to have big ideas in order to start writing. We can start right in with the chores, with the laundry, with the messiness of our lives. We can focus and be fully awake, no matter what we are doing. We need to learn to create room *within* our lives, not outside of them, in order to expand the space for both spirituality and writing.

Holly

I'm at Campbell Nelson Volkswagen repair shop, waiting for new glow plugs to be installed in my VW Golf. It's taking longer than I expected, so after reading every article in the tattered copy of the *Seattle Post-Intelligencer*, I turn my attention to the signs on the wall. Normally, I'd skip the mission statement—they all sound the same—but something makes me read this one. "To encourage, equip, and engage one another with love to meet the needs of our co-workers, customers, and community." *With love.* Right there in the mission statement. And so far, everything I've experienced suggests that it could be true: They *have* treated me with something resembling love.

First, when I called yesterday, Ryan, the mechanic who answered, said, "Yes, we're busy, but we'll fit you in," because he knew new glow plugs would make a big difference in our diesel Golf starting this week, since temperatures have plummeted into the twenties. When I meet Ryan today, he is as friendly in person as he'd been on the phone. He remembers me, makes sure I am comfortable. I watch as he greets everyone with warmth and his full attention, as he goes carefully through each work order to make sure we understand what will be done on our vehicles. These small acts of kindness matter, whether they are part of a mission statement or not.

Observing this, I'm reminded of Right Livelihood, one aspect of the Buddha's Eight-Fold Path. As Thich Nhat Hanh puts it in *The Heart of the Buddha's Teaching*, "To practice Right Livelihood (*samyag ajiva*), you have to find a way to earn your living without transgressing your ideals of love and compassion. The way you support yourself can be an expression of your deepest self, or it can be a source of suffering for you and others." Clearly, this is Right Work for Ryan; clearly, he loves not just his customers but also his vocation. I'm struck by how many forms Right Livelihood can take. We are tempted to elevate certain kinds of work—the community organizer, the teacher in a depressed socioeconomic area, the hospice worker, the doctor, the nurse—but Right Livelihood can be any work that is performed with a full heart.

I think of the delicious, hearty bread baked by the monks at Deer Park Monastery, who rose at 4 a.m. so we could enjoy it, steaming, as we lined up for breakfast each morning in the cool hour before the sun rose. I'm reminded, too, of my friend Judith in Indianola, who bakes bread each week, then delivers it, still warm, to each customer in a brown paper bag with the customer's name on it, written in her beautiful, careful script. Each week I open the bag and am surprised by its contents—sourdough whole wheat, rosemary, Parmesan, sun-dried tomato—I love them all. This week the sourdough whole wheat bread was not quite oblong, not quite round; the loaf had risen unevenly and that made me love it all the more.

In her poem "The Piemaker," Lin Max describes in detail the act of making pies with attention and love, and through this attention arriving at that still point in her world. She acknowledges her initial imperfect state of mind, the resistance to doing it "right," but then goes beyond that to understand why she perseveres.

> Still in my nightgown I would go down
> to the kitchen where the first sun slanted
> across the linoleum in sweet silence
> and begin cutting cold butter into sifted flour
> rocking the pastry cutter rhythmically,
> until it resembled coarse cornmeal.
>
> I always wanted to quit too soon
> resisting the monotonous repetition,

attention wandering wild, but it always
needs to be much finer, the granitic
sand of the high Sierra, and it takes
time.   It takes time.

. . . I always thought I'd have little girls
and be a good mother, be the mother

I never had, teach them how to make pies
and how to get past wanting to quit, show them
the place in our minds beyond the last ridge
where we can rock the cutter endlessly,
the place where there is no time and how to
tightly crimp the edge with alternating thumbs.

    Maybe, when we do all our work with this kind of attention, time does stand still; maybe it even expands. We've all felt the magic of reaching this place of "no time": when it happens, we feel more productive, more engaged, more deeply satisfied.

    Soon, Ryan will return with the key to my Golf. He'll calmly run through the work done. He'll tell me that the mechanics replaced all four glow plugs and didn't charge any additional labor: "We were in there anyway—we might as well replace them all." I'll happily write my check and thank him, re-reading the mission statement one more time as I head out the door. My car will start easily for the first time in weeks, and I'll head for the ferry, grateful for people like Ryan who do their work with a full heart, reminding me that there are many ways to be engaged in the world, to do work that matters, with love.

Contemplation Practices

1. The next time you're in a waiting room or in a line at a store, put down the magazine or the cell phone or your daily planner, and instead observe what is going on around you. Commit to doing this for five, ten, or fifteen minutes. Especially observe the people who are working: *How* do they do their work? What kind of atmosphere do they create with their attention or lack of attention?

2. Reflect on Right Livelihood. Is your work Right Livelihood? What would you need to change to make it so for you? Think about how you might engage in your work with a full heart. Reflect on others who you feel are engaged in Right Livelihood. What can you learn from their example?

3. The next time you have a big chore to do—especially one you consider onerous—pretend you have a spiritual being at your side, pitching in. This being can be any person, deity, or thing that acts as an ally to help you be your better self. It could be an ancestor or a child or an animal. What happens if you allow this chore to be an opportunity for mindfulness or contemplation?

Writing Practices

1. Write about your observation in the waiting room or in line. Describe the small sensory details (what do you see, smell, hear?). As you're writing, does anything unexpected comes up? Why do you remember the details you do? What memories do they evoke? What do they spur you to say about your life?

2. Write a description of your work for someone who is not familiar with it. Use the vocabulary of your profession, defining the words in context. Try to discover the beauty in what has become ordinary for you. "The Navigational Fix" is an example of a poem that uses the language of navigation as a unifying metaphor. It is from Holly's chapbook, *Boxing the Compass*.

> For a good fix, we need two lines, 45 degrees
> apart, to meet, one leg of the dividers anchored
>
> the other swinging on its arc until
> the lines intersect, X saying here—
>
> this moment wrenched from time, plumbed
> in place. I spread the dividers' metal legs,
>
> measure degrees in seconds, minutes, hours,
> gauge *speed made good*, prick one small foot,
>
> drag its lead twin in an arc, an easy pivot.
> Then the next. Take a bearing off the lighthouse,
>
> another arc, and where the two overlap
> a sprawling X   but already we've moved on.

3. Using the Campbell Nelson VW mission statement as a model, write a mission statement for yourself, describing how you would like to engage with your writing and your community. Begin by writing key words or phrases that explain succinctly the qualities you would most like to embody, then work them into a statement of positive intention. It doesn't have to be grand or noble, just authentic. Come back to this mission statement from time to

time and assess how you're doing. Are you living up to it? If not, what are the obstacles that get in the way? (You could also do this with others, as a family, or in a writing group.)

4. Think about a hobby or other work you do—like Lin Max's pie making—and describe all the actions you take as you perform this activity. How might this activity be a form of contemplation?

5. Write a history of yourself through a history of your work. What jobs have you held that felt deeply satisfying? Why were they satisfying? Consider all jobs, including ones you did as a small child.

6. Write a parody or imitation of Billy Collins's poem "Shoveling Snow with Buddha," substituting your own chore and your own ally. For example: "Vacuuming with Jesus," or "Washing Dishes with my Great-Grandmother."

7. Write a poem or short prose piece that begins with the first line of the poem "To Be of Use" by Marge Piercy: "The people I love best. . . ." Who are the people you love best? What images come to mind? How does this line lead you to consider what's really important to you? It could lead you somewhere completely unexpected. Take, as an example, "Trying" by Nancy Pagh, which was inspired by and modeled after Piercy's poem:

> The people I love best are the ones who try: the aged who rise
> early each damp morning and part the clump of coffee filters
> with arthritic fingers—and the others who stay up
> late after working all day in retail, hot pink curl of ear
> pressing the receiver, listening to the friend who is selfish

but in agony now. I love the men who are fathers
to children, not buddies not video-game rivals not boys
themselves but clumsy men who ache over the fragility of sons,
but preserve the fragility of sons despite what everyone says.
I love those who feel no skill has come to them innate,
who will hold their small inland dogs again and again
above the sea on vacation, to watch in amazement
the knowing animal body that paddles through air. I love
the B+ student. The thick-chinned girl always picked
fourth when choosing sides for the softball team.
The lover who says it first. The lover who says it second
after a long, long pause. The lover who says it knowing
the answer is no, no, I am too broken. People who knit
things together. People willing to take things apart
and roll all the strands of yarn into new balls for next time.
The woman who loaded her backseat full of blankets and drove
for three days to the hurricane site. Even the loafer who tries
his mother's patience, who quietly speculates and eventually
decodes the universe for us all. Believe me, I have tried
to love others, the meager personalities who charm and butter,
the jaded the cynics the players and floaters all safe
in their cages, this life no responsibility they can own.
They see it too—how trying is always a risk,
a kind of vulnerability some choose for ourselves because
our fathers taught us well, our fathers taught us to try
to remain as fragile and full as this world that loves us.

Eight

The Moments in Between

Help me to love a slow progression,
to have no prejudice
that up is better than down or vice versa.
Help me to enjoy the in-between.
 —Gunilla Norris, "Climbing Stairs"

Brenda

I'm on my way home from a short vacation on San Juan Island. Soon I'll be zooming up I-5 to go pick up my dog, Abbe, from the boarding kennel, and when I get home, I'll be caught up in short order with all the tasks that have piled up in my absence. I'll be making lists (well, to be honest, I've already made a list, a *long* one), and I'll begin methodically making my way through it, forgetting much of the slow spaciousness I had on the island, the time to simply think, or really just to *be*.

So I have a choice here. I can either start now with all my busyness, my mind planning and worrying and projecting, or this time betwixt and between can be a breather, another opportunity for mindfulness, for contemplation, perhaps even for writing. We spend a great deal of lives in these in-between stretches of time; what we do with them just might determine the tenor of our lives.

Perhaps a commute on an LA freeway or sitting in close quarters on an airplane stuck on the runway does not feel so ripe a time for contemplation. But one of my teachers, Jack Duffy, has said that a powerful practice can be "sitting-in-the-car meditation," being fully present to the mass of humanity surrounding you, feeling yourself an inextricable part of it, rather than separate from it. He teaches that just taking a few moments to breathe at any transition—getting in the car, before you turn the key in the ignition, for example—will profoundly change your life.

Thich Nhat Hanh asks us to practice "stopping" meditation at a red light, grateful for this opportunity to simply sit and be, rather than trying to get someplace else. The red light is a bell of mindfulness, cheerfully telling us to truly stop. He also asks us to practice "ringing telephone" meditation, stopping to breathe for three breaths before answering.

These teachers know the value of such little snatches of time, the myriad opportunities for contemplation and mindfulness, even when we think we're too busy for such things. One of my steadiest practices for years has been my "walking to work" meditation, the eight minutes it takes me to walk from my parking place to my office. It's now become a habit: As soon as I turn off the car and before I unlatch my seat belt, I allow myself just ten seconds to take a deep breath and exhale. That one breath "resets" me, and when I get out of the car, hoisting my heavy bag over my shoulder, I'm already a bit more present, a bit more ready for the day ahead. I practice walking meditation—walking not too slowly but at a measured pace, trying to be aware of all that surrounds me. Of course, my mind wanders, planning my classes or a difficult conversation I need to have with a colleague or student, but the practice of mindfulness is simply a practice of noticing: When I notice my mind wandering, I come back to my steps, and to my breath, sometimes silently using the verse Thich Nhat Hanh suggests: "I have arrived, I am home" with each step.

Even when I do this for just a minute, I feel my mind settle, and I'm more ready to do my work.

I'm lucky that on my particular walk I have a view of Bellingham Bay, so I have the opportunity to notice its continually changing countenance—how it is, of course, steadily *there* throughout every season, but how the face of it changes: sometimes placid and smooth as glass, sometimes choppy and topped with whitecaps. Sometimes it's green and sometimes it's blue. It is what it is—as are our days: unpredictable and beautiful. Our job is simply to pay attention—not judging, not interpreting, but allowing it all in.

Holly

I ride the Edmonds-Kingston ferry to work almost every day, so these are familiar waters. Over the twenty years I've been teaching, I've come to value my time on the ferry as an opportunity to reflect, read, and sometimes even to write. I value it as a reminder to be present to whatever the day brings. It must be deeply engrained from my seasons working on the sea in Alaska, because I still pay attention to the weather—today, wind blowing twenty-five out of the southeast—and the birds—a few pelagic cormorants on the pilings, then the seagulls that soar alongside, sometimes looking in as if to check up on us. In the morning, I head east into a pink-streaked sunrise over the Cascade range; in the evening, if we're lucky, we glide into a gold sunset, the Olympic Mountains etched in stark relief.

Since this ferry ride is now my only regular chance to be on the water, I look forward to this passage each day, whatever moments of wild and unpredictable beauty it might bring—sometimes even in the form of true wildness: the dark fins of a wandering pod of orcas, the sleek head of a lone seal tucked in the waves.

Passage. We typically use that word to refer to sea journeys. But it's good to remind ourselves that each time we set off for another destination we are making a small journey, and that we need to prepare for it, as we would any passage.

Most of my rituals are mundane, pragmatic: I look for a table by the window on the starboard side (close to the women's bathroom—that's the pragmatic aspect), fill my green metal traveling mug with hot water, drop in a Yogi tea bag, and while it steeps, I write in my journal. Some days I scribble down a few images, maybe an overheard conversation, maybe just a question. Other days I'll write the entire time, sometimes even end up with the draft of a poem. Here's a journal entry from last spring, which may or may not find its way into a poem:

This afternoon, the blue heron balances on a strand of bull kelp, motionless, waiting for a fish to swim past. I watch as the next ferry grows larger on the horizon, draws closer, and still, not a feather moves. May I be as still, as focused.

I have the poet Linda Bierds to thank for this practice. Years ago, when I was lucky enough to study with her, she told us about her notebook, how she uses it as a way of keeping connected to images and writing, even when she doesn't have time to actually write. Since then, I've carried my journal with me each day on the ferry, recording what I see, overheard snatches of conversations, odd newspaper stories, all which might someday become seeds for poems or essays.

My colleague Sue also rides the ferry, and some days we end up on the same boat. Over the years, we've learned how to give each other space, to enjoy being together in silence as we both grade papers or, better, write in our notebooks. Some rare days, when we're both caught up on our work, we've even been able to share our poems or other writing—and that's the best passage of all.

Some passages are marked by solitude and concentration—papers to return in an hour—and some by camaraderie—writing with a good friend. But each passage reminds me, again, that life happens in these in-between times and places, like the messy littoral zone where sea meets land. Even now, as the engines slow to a quiet hum and we coast toward the creosote-soaked pilings, the sun unexpectedly spurts through the clouds and gleams across the water, a beacon shining us home.

Contemplation Practices

1. Try practicing walking meditation as you walk from your car to your work-place or from your car to the grocery store. You don't need to walk too slowly; simply be aware of each step and of the sensory input around you. Feel your foot touching the pavement, the movement of your body. Breathe in and breathe out. You can do this for as short a time as one minute to feel the effects. You can use Thich Nhat Hanh's phrase—"I have arrived, I am home"—to measure your steps, or any other phrase that resonates for you: "Here, now" is a simple one, or "Step one, step two."

2. Any time you have a habitual few moments that are part of a transition, use this for a time of "stopping" and mindfulness. Breathe in and out mindfully for three full breaths. Observe the people around you with compassion.

3. The next time you're at a red light, try "stopping" meditation: Let go of impatience and use this time as an opportunity to simply rest in the moment. Or the next time your cell phone rings, try practicing "ringing telephone" meditation and breathe three times before answering it.

4. The next time you have a layover at an airport, resist the temptation to fill your time with eating, shopping, talking on your cell phone, or working on your computer. Simply sit. Simply breathe. Or do a walking meditation up and down the concourse. Observe the people around you. Take this time to practice.

5. Ride the ferry, or the train, or the bus without a destination, just for the pleasure of the passage.

Writing Practices

1. Write about your daily commute, even if this commute is just from one room to another in your house. What are your little rituals and preparations? What do you observe along the way? What remains consistent and what changes?

2. Write about a bigger transition in your life. Try to focus on one scene that shows you betwixt and between phases in your life. What can you learn about yourself in this moment of transition? Was it a graceful transition or an awkward one? How can you embrace the imperfections?

3. Carry a small notebook with you so that whenever you have some waiting time, you can use it to write. This could be waiting at the doctor's office, waiting at the curb for your child to get out of school, or waiting for a friend to arrive at the coffee shop. If you make it a habit to turn to writing to pass these few minutes—even if it's just to practice writing down details, observations, a bit of news that caught your attention—you will find your writing mind waking up in the most unexpected places.

4. If you commute by bus, train, or ferry, try using your commuting time to write. Start out by practicing "eavesdropping meditation," writing down stray bits of conversation to see if you can shape them into a poem or short essay. Or simply observe the people around you and write down salient details, as Rebecca McClanahan does in "Early Morning, Downtown 1 Train":

In this car packed with closed faces, this tube
    of light tunneling through darkness: two sleeping boys, so close
        I could touch them without reaching—their smooth brown faces,

planed cheekbones like Peruvian steppes leading from
    or to some beautiful ruin. Boys so alike they must be brothers.
        And the small, worried man they sprawl against, too young to seem

so old: father. How far have they come? How far to go?
    They sleep as only loved children sleep, wholly, no need
        to tighten or clutch, to fold themselves in. Their heads are thrown
          back,

mouths open—no, agape, which looks like *agape*,
    the highest form of love, some minister told me long ago.
        As if love is a cupboard of lower and higher shelves, and why bother

reaching if you have hands like the hands of this young father,
    cracked and blistered, stamped with the pattern of shovel or pick.
        For someone must do our digging, and rise in the dark to dress

the children carefully, as these boys are dressed, and pack their knapsacks,
    and ease out of the seat without waking the open-mouthed
        younger one nor the older whose head now rests fully

on the emptied seat . . . but, "My, God," I think
    as the brakes squeal and the father moves quickly to face the door,
      "he is leaving
        these children, a father leaving his children." The train slows at 50th

and he presses his body against the door, lifting his arms
    above his head—a signal? surrender?—as the door slides open
      and a woman steps in, small and dark like the father, her body

lost in a white uniform. She touches his sleeve, something
    passes between their eyes. Not sadness exactly, but ragged
      exhaustion, frayed edges meeting: his night her day, her night

his day, goodbye hello. She slides onto the seat, lifting
    one son's head to her lap. His mouth is still open, his body limp.
      She smoothes his collar. Her small hands move to his lips,

closing them gently the way one closes the mouth
    of the recently dead. But the boy is not dead. Just sleeping,
      an arm thrown over his brother. His mother near.

Nine

Reviving Spiritual Traditions

My coming to faith did not start with a leap but rather a series of staggers from what seemed like one safe place to another. Like lily pads, round and green, these places summoned and then held me up while I grew.

—Anne Lamott, *Traveling Mercies*

Brenda

I always look forward to celebrating the Jewish New Year. Rosh Hashanah—and the ten days of reflection leading to Yom Kippur, the day of atonement—is a time of renewal as the season turns into fall. I make brisket roasted in wine and apricots for my friends, and we eat honey cake to ensure a sweet year ahead. We walk together at sunset to a creek in my neighborhood park, and there we throw in breadcrumbs symbolic of the sins we'd like to let go—reenacting a ritual performed over centuries by my ancestors. We articulate our aspirations for the coming year as the creek cheerfully washes our sins away.

Thich Nhat Hanh and the Dalai Lama both encourage us to go back to the religious traditions of our families and childhoods, to find in these traditions the core truths and practices that can deeply support us. We are not separate from our ancestors; we are made of them, figuratively and literally. If we can find our way back with an open heart, we might find new connections that will surprise us.

When I was a child, the New Year meant boring services in the synagogue, the adults uncomfortable in their fancy clothes, the smell of roast chicken and brisket following us everywhere. We sat for hours in the hard pews of the sanctuary, listening to the rabbi and the cantor and the congregation plead to God for absolution. This God was an angry God, and we had to be very good, had to plead our case to be written into the "Book of Life" for the coming year. The services, and the holiday itself, seemed to be about guilt (well, of course—we were *Jewish*, after all!), and on Yom Kippur, the last day of the ten-day ritual, we were admonished to fast to purify ourselves in God's eyes. I didn't take in much, but I did know it was one more opportunity for failure, to be guilty for my own shortcomings.

But several years ago, I found myself in a progressive synagogue, and as we read the Torah portions together, the word *forgiveness* stood out this time. I began to see that this holiday is really more about forgiveness than guilt. And the rabbi, Ted Falcon, urged us to see this as a time to write *ourselves* into the Book of Life. "It's not about literally who is going to live and who is going to die," he said. "That would be too easy. It's about either being truly alive to your life, or being dead to your life. We are given the dignity of responsibility to choose."

The Jewish New Year, I realized then, could be a time to sincerely assess our actions of the year past and to make promises to ourselves for the year ahead. We can contemplate ourselves with honesty, but without judgment. We can write down what we would like to let go of, and we can let it go. We can become who we truly are, because, as Rabbi Falcon put it, "The world needs *you*, just as you are."

Powerful writing can emerge from reflecting on our spiritual traditions in the light of what we've come to value most strongly; we can see what kernels of truth have carried over into our adult lives, sometimes transformed in unexpected ways. For example, Rebecca Solnit begins her book *A Field Guide to Getting Lost* with this anecdote: "The first time I got drunk was on Elijah's wine. I was eight or so. It was Passover, the feast that celebrates the flight from Egypt and invites the prophet into the house." She goes on to describe the details of the tablecloth, the stemmed goblet, then:

> I don't know if the rest of the tradition was followed and a door left open for him to enter by, but I can picture the orange front door or one of the sliding glass doors into the backyard of this ranch-style house in a small valley open to the cool night air of spring. Ordinarily, we locked doors, though nothing unexpected came down our street in this northernmost subdivision in the county but wildlife, deer tap-tapping on the asphalt in the early hours, raccoons and skunks hiding in the shrubbery. This opening the door to night, prophecy, and the end of time would have been a thrilling violation of ordinary practice. Nor can I recall what the wine opened up for me—perhaps a happier detachment from the conversation going on above me, a sense of limpidness in the suddenly tangible gravity of a small body on this middle-sized planet.
>
> Leave the door open for the unknown, the door into the dark. That's where the most important things come from, where you yourself came from, and where you will go.

Notice how Solnit allows herself to imagine her way back into the details of that early childhood experience, and she cues the reader into this act of imagination. And only through imagining does she hone in on the one detail—the open door—that will lead her into a philosophical rumination that will carry her entire book. What happens when we open the door to the unknown? What kinds of danger and pleasures wait to greet us?

Holly

I grew up in a small town in Minnesota where my family belonged to the Congregational Church—"the Congo," we called it as kids. My early memories of church are of watching colorful prisms of light from the stained glass windows flutter across the ceiling during a too-long sermon, then coffee and cookies in the parlor, where I once wrapped my arms around the knees of a woman who turned out not to be my mother. Of course, I remember the singing, all the familiar hymns, and the day when at last I was trusted to hold the heavy red leather hymnal myself. I remember how I loved the Christmas Eve candlelight service, when we'd all file out into the dark, cold December night singing "Silent Night," cupping candles in wax cups, their glow illuminating our faces, until the time Nancy Edstrom's hair caught on fire and we switched to safer, less romantic electric candles.

Even as a kid, I liked the sense of community, the friends I'd see each Sunday at church or in the summer at church picnics. Each week I'd proudly put fifty cents of my precious allowance in the heavy offering plate, knowing my money would be spent to feed children in Africa or some other worthy project. Church for me was singing hymns, community, and "helping others less fortunate," as my mother reminded us each week.

Elizabeth Andrew, in her book *Writing the Sacred Journey*, writes: "Every religious tradition has some dimension that captures the imagination of children and touches their essential being." Looking back on that time now, I know that something touched my essential being—maybe the singing or the stained-glass windows—but it didn't seem to be God. In fact, it never occurred to me that my Congregational faith was intended to connect me to God, no matter how many sermons I sat through (though I admit to some curiosity about the Holy Ghost). Community, yes, but God was so much more elusive, glimpsed only alone, in solitude, usually outdoors.

It was at the YMCA camp in northern Minnesota I attended each summer that I began to develop a relationship with this elusive presence. There, on a small outcropping of rocks looking out over Little Boy Lake, we'd put together our own Sunday church services, which usually consisted of reading E.E. Cummings poems and singing Joan Baez and Pete Seeger folk songs. *Ah*, I remember thinking, *maybe* this *is a God I can understand.* There, and on ten-day canoe trips into the Canadian Quetico, as we paddled across smooth blue lakes, watching clouds drift across the sky, that whisper of a voice began to speak more clearly, connecting me to my inner life, a life I'd found before only in the pages of a book.

I managed to keep up the outward appearance of a religious tradition only because I attended a Lutheran college where attendance at daily chapel services was required. Even though it seemed a much more dogmatic religion than the one I'd known, I didn't mind; all the things I loved were still there, even if I had to sit through liturgy to enjoy them. The chapel was built of maple and birch and there were plenty of stained-glass windows to distract me during the twenty minutes of worship, not to mention the transcendent voices of the St. Olaf choir. I drew the line at communion, though—I felt too much of a hypocrite to stand before the pastor with my mouth open, waiting to take the wafer, drink from the chalice, without believing in my heart that this was the body and blood of Christ, even symbolically.

After I'd been fishing in Alaska for several seasons, I reconnected with that elusive spirit I'd experienced as we paddled in silence across still, depthless blue lakes. I found I could re-enter that timeless place I loved as we ran to our next destination, and I tracked our progress with a penciled track line on the chart, all my thoughts swept aside to concentrate only on the question: *Where, exactly, are we?*

In the meantime, I'd stumbled upon Buddhism through poetry; I'd begun to read Gary Snyder, Kenneth Rexroth, and Robert Sund. In particular, I was given a beautiful letterpress chapbook by Robert Sund, *As Though the Word Blue Had Been Dropped into the Water,* that I carried with me for a year, discovering that, like the natural world, his brief, koan-like poems fed my spirit. I was in graduate school in English, struggling with understanding—and accepting—the theory of deconstruction, when I read his poem "Like a Boat Drifting."

> Like a boat drifting,
> sleep flows forward
>   on the deep water of dreams.
> Drifts and drifts . . .
> until, finally
> the bottom falls out of knowledge.
>
> In the fragrant mist of dawn
> the rower wakes,
>   picks up the oars, sets them,
>   and begins to row.
> All night
> he labored in his dream
>   to be born
> like a song in the mouth of God.

Fed up with dry academic theories, I was ready to let the bottom fall out of knowledge, more than ready "to be born / like a song in the mouth of God." In reading Snyder and Sund, I found that poetry itself could provide entry into this world of spirit, as I branched out to other spiritual traditions, represented in the works of poets such as Tu Fu, Li Po, Rilke, Rumi, and Hafiz. I then gravitated to the growing number of contemporary poets whose poems speak to the spirit, among them some of the voices you hear in this book: Denise Levertov, Jane Hirshfield, Tess Gallagher, Sam Green, Robert Hass, W. S. Merwin, William Stafford, and Jane Kenyon.

Whatever our spiritual traditions, whether born into or acquired, they help shape us. Perhaps we continue to practice them, with love and growing understanding. Perhaps we refine our own spirituality by pushing against doctrine; or we might leave these traditions to search out other practices that better speak to our essential nature, following the whiff of that elusive presence.

Contemplation Practices

1. If you no longer participate fully in the religion of your youth, is there a way you can take some small aspect or ritual of that religion and reconfigure it in a way that's meaningful for you today?

2. If you do still participate in the religion of your youth, reflect on what aspects of this religion speak most strongly to you today. How has this connection changed as you mature?

3. Visit a place of worship for "research" purposes. Observe the rituals, the community, from a relaxed stance of watchfulness, without judgment, paying attention to your own breath and body. What resonates for you? What small details seem significant or rich for your writing?

4. Search out the writers and poets who articulate your complex spiritual beliefs in ways that speak to you. Start a collection of such writings and use them as part of your personal practice. Attend readings in your community to hear new work that might become part of your collection.

Writing Practices

1. Write about your earliest memory of religion or spirituality. Write it as a specific scene, using sensory imagery. As Andre Dubus III says in his introduction to *The Best Spiritual Writing, 2001*: "Great soul is found in art and all of its concrete, specific, and sensual particulars. . . . It seems to me that no writing can approach the truly spiritual until it seeks to evoke the lowly terrain of the soul and the body that holds it." Try to avoid lofty or abstract words and concentrate instead on the physical details of the scene, as Rebecca Solnit did in her passage on Elijah's wine.

2. Write more scenes spurred by this early memory, working your way toward adulthood. What themes seem to be prevalent? Keep pushing at the images that resonate with you.

3. Write about your early spiritual tradition and how it shapes your beliefs today. Are there rituals that seemed meaningless then that have since acquired meaning? How does this tradition inform your current spiritual practice?

4. In *Traveling Mercies*, Anne Lamott describes her spiritual path this way:

   > When I look back at some of these early resting places—the boisterous home of the Catholics, the soft armchair of the Christian Science mom, adoption by ardent Jews—I can see how flimsy and indirect a path they made. Yet each step brought me closer to the verdant pad of faith on which I somehow stay afloat today.

   Write about your own series of "resting places."

Ten

Eating as Contemplative Practice

It is more fun to talk with someone who doesn't use long, difficult words but rather short, easy words like "What about lunch?"

—Winnie the Pooh

Brenda

For me (as for many Jewish kids), my family and religious memories are really all about food. I remember the brisket and the latkes at Hanukkah, the roast chickens brought out on big platters at every holiday. I remember the matzo at Passover, and the care package my grandmother sent from New York, filled with kosher mandelbrot and jellied fruits covered in chocolate. She made us egg creams when we visited: an odd concoction of milk, chocolate syrup, and seltzer water (not sure where the "egg" part came in). She cooked meals that took hours and hours, set quivering gefilte fish down on the table, bought marble rye at the bakery down the block.

Now, as an adult, I think about food all the time, planning my next meal even while I'm eating the one in front of me. Once, on a meditation retreat, we had gorgeous blueberries every morning, picked fresh from my teacher's bushes—heirloom plants, handed down from her mother and grandmother.

These blueberries were sweet and complex, each one bursting with the essence of true blueberry. Eating them became another form of meditation, the most enjoyable moment in my day. Afterward, I wrote a little poem to share with the community at the tea ceremony:

> Even as I eat each blueberry
> from my bowl, I find myself
> craving more blueberries.

Everyone laughed. Everyone, it turned out, did exactly the same thing. Delicious food wakes up our senses—wakes us up to ourselves—and since eating is something we do frequently (some of us more frequently than others!), it becomes one more opportunity for mindful awareness and can provide so much powerful material for writing.

When I joined Weight Watchers to take off the twenty-five pounds that had snuck onto my body, I managed to take them off in a few months' time, not only by rigorously following the plan, but by remembering to recite the "Five Contemplations" Thich Nhat Hanh asks us to say before each meal. These verses are found in his book *Present Moment, Wonderful Moment*:

~ This food is the gift of the whole universe, the earth, the sky and much hard work.
~ May I eat in mindfulness so as to be worthy to receive it.
~ May I transform my unskillful states of mind and learn to eat in moderation.
~ May I take only food that nourishes and prevents illness.
~ I accept this food to realize the path of understanding and love.

By taking this half-minute to stop before eating my food—to fully appreciate the meal on my plate—I was able to be satisfied with much less and also able to enjoy it more fully. When with others, if I felt shy about saying the contemplations out loud, I said them silently to myself. But sometimes I suggested we all say them together, and I found that most people, especially children, really enjoyed these few moments of appreciation.

Thich Nhat Hanh stresses mindful eating as an essential part of any contemplative practice. Here is his famous "eating an orange meditation" that appeared in his article "The Moment is Perfect":

Take the time to eat an orange in mindfulness. If you eat an orange in forgetfulness, caught in your anxiety and sorrow, the orange is not really there. But if you bring your mind and body together to produce true presence, you can see that the orange is a miracle. Peel the orange. Smell the fruit. See the orange blossoms in the orange, and the rain and the sun that have gone through the orange blossoms. The orange tree that has taken several months to bring this wonder to you. Put a section in your mouth, close your mouth mindfully, and with mindfulness feel the juice coming out of the orange. Taste the sweetness. Do you have the time to do so? If you think you don't have time to eat an orange like this, what are you using that time for? Are you using your time to worry or using your time to live?

Once we experience our food fully, we'll be able to write about it in original ways. Li-Young Lee's poem "Eating Together" is a wonderful example of mindful awareness of food, and the poem shows how a clear focus on a simple meal can be the springboard to contemplating something much bigger—in this case, his father's death:

In the steamer is the trout
seasoned with slivers of ginger,
two sprigs of green onion, and sesame oil.
We shall eat it with rice for lunch,
brothers, sister, my mother who will
taste the sweetest meat of the head,
holding it between her fingers
deftly, the way my father did
weeks ago. Then he lay down
to sleep like a snow-covered road
winding through pines older than him,
without any travelers, and lonely for no one.

Notice how Lee begins with concrete observations of this simple meal. He directs our attention, turns our gaze toward the table: Look, he says, "In the steamer is the trout." He notes every small detail, an act of attention that elevates this meal and shows the speaker's investment in looking at it fully: It's not just any fish but a trout, not just green onion but "two sprigs" of green onion, small details that make us pay attention and show us how closely he is looking.

He then shows us what will happen in the next few moments: "We shall eat it with rice for lunch": a predictable act, comforting in its predictability. The meal shows the family in communion together, and invokes the one important member who is absent: the father. The mother's "deft" handling of the fish head links the family to the father, and in this way, the speaker of the poem is able to both celebrate his father's presence at the table—through the food the father had eaten so many times during his life—and quietly grieve his absence.

Lee comes a long way in a short amount of time. In just twelve lines we experience not only this beautiful trout but his love for his family. By paying attention with such care, we can tap into the store of memories and emotions food can hold—for ourselves and for others.

Holly

Growing up, I hated beets. In Minnesota, they were mostly served pickled, as a garnish, not in their sweet, unadulterated glory. I'd dutifully take one bite, then push them off to the side. Later, when I was older, my grandmother would serve them for lunch, cold slices arranged on a plate, covered with some kind of yellow sauce—hollandaise? I'd take a few bites, then push the plate away. But now, fall means boiling beets for beet, arugula, and goat cheese salad, or roasting them slowly in their jackets, olive oil rubbed on to soften their skins, then tossed with sea salt.

I get these beets, and many other vegetables, from Persephone Farm, just up the road from my cabin in Indianola. For six seasons now, I've been a subscriber to a community-supported agriculture (or CSA) program, in which I and others pay in advance for the produce of the growing season. That way, the farm has operating capital to plant the crops and we, the subscribers, are guaranteed a share of the harvest. Each Wednesday afternoon, armed with my straw basket and canvas bags, I walk ten minutes from my house to the farm. Fox always comes with me on this expedition, eager to sniff out any voles or shrews in the tall grasses lining the road. We like to walk up the trail, not the road, for the trail takes us on a rich olfactory tour through the lavender beds, up past the onions and garlic, past the strawberry beds, by the compost piles, and finally, by the old potting shed.

The shed is lined with boxes of produce, filled and waiting to be picked up. I'm early today, one of the first to arrive, and the wood boxes are overflowing with a few remnants of summer's harvest—late ears of corn, tomatoes, and a variety of squash: delicata, acorn, a few ornamental gourds. I swing open the door of the walk-in cooler to see what's there: salad greens, chard, broccoli rabe. Now my favorite part: choosing a bouquet of flowers. This time of year, sunflowers always win and I choose those that have deep burgundy centers called, fittingly, autumn sonata. Then I pick up a recipe for fixing delicata squash with pesto and pine nuts, chat with Molly and Zack, the apprentices who will be finishing up the season at the end of the month, and head back down the trail.

As I put away my week's bounty, I feel lucky that I can walk to fetch my food, that it's grown just up the road by friends, that each week, with very little effort, I can eat what's local and in season. Friends inevitably ask: What if you receive something you don't like, such as radishes? Or too many zucchini? It's true; this happens. I still don't like radishes, but I am learning to appreciate the color and zing they add when grated lightly into a green salad. I've found a recipe for chocolate cake that, amazingly, calls for several cups of grated zucchini. Each week, I'm reminded to be grateful for what I've been given and to find ways to make use of it, even if that means finding or inventing recipes for foods I might have avoided in the past.

Like fava beans. They're big, fleshy beans, and the first time I served them, simply, boiled and chilled in a salad, they received mixed reviews. But John broke out the food processor and started throwing ingredients together. Now we look forward to our fava-feta tapenade, made by boiling the fava beans, then mashing them with feta cheese, olive oil, lemon, and just a hint of garlic. Each week, this practice reminds me to try to do the same with my life—to accept what I'm given, then be creative with how to use it. I might be surprised by what I've overlooked.

When I travel, I'm heartened to see the growth in farmers' markets in many cities and towns around the country—so one doesn't need to be a member of a CSA to enjoy eating locally, to meet the farmer who dug your red beets out of the earth. For me, it's easier to eat mindfully when I know where my food came from, know how hard my farming friends are working. I enjoy my food more when I'm conscious of how my food choices affect both the land and the people who work the land.

Contemplation Practices

1. If you're so inclined, say a grace before eating. This could be a traditional grace from a religious tradition, or something like the Five Contemplations from Thich Nhat Hanh's tradition. It doesn't need to be solemn, nor does it need to use religious language. Make it your own, and notice how this practice might change your eating habits. David Gunderson's "Meal Gatha" is an example of a grace, or *gatha*, from the Buddhist tradition:

   > With gratitude and joy
   > we receive this gift of food.
   > Into ourselves we take
   > these changing forms of light
   > through which we will be changed:
   > other bodies becoming
   > our body,
   > other life becoming
   > our life;
   > that there is
   > one body
   > one life
   > shared by all
   > we vow to remember.

2. Try Thich Nhat Hanh's "eating an orange" meditation, using an orange, a pomegranate, or any other food you like (chocolate's a good one!). Explore this food with all your senses.

Writing Practices

1. After doing an eating meditation, write about the food you ate, creating a poem or a prose poem that describes this food in new and unexpected ways. How does this food connect you with the contemplative or writing mind?

2. Write about a specific food from your childhood that was a key part of your family's identity or culture. Write in specific detail, evoking not only the food but the community that partook of it.

3. Write about a food you hated as a kid that you now love. Is there anything metaphorical in this conversion?

4. Gather many different foods that you love and lay them out on a table. Experience these things with all your senses: See them, smell them, touch them, taste them, listen as they make contact with the table or your mouth. Begin a poem or a prose piece simply by listing all that you experience with this food, as Pattiann Rogers does in this excerpt from her poem "Service with Benediction":

> Chunk honey, creamed honey, buckwheat
> honey on buckwheat bread—like glass lanterns,
> there's enough concentrated summer sun caught
> in these jars of comb honey to give us

ample light to travel by on a winter night.

Sesame breads, sausage breads, almond
breads, sweet panettones, cassava cakes
and millet cakes, all are laid out
on the table before me beside these bowls
of molasses honey and heather honey, wild-
wood honey, gathered by wild bees, hallows
of honey, orisons of bulging loaves.

So I eat sun and earth by the slice. . . .

5. In a poem or a short piece of prose, begin by describing, in concrete, simple
    detail, a meal that you make frequently. Follow Li-Young Lee's progression
    in "Eating Together": begin fully in the present moment, then show what
    will happen in the next few moments: Who will be eating this meal? What
    are the circumstances? Then, if the language and details seem to allow it,
    invoke what is absent at this meal. See if you can maintain a steady attention
    to the details to see where they will lead. Try this several times, with different
    foods, to see what happens.

Eleven

On Gratitude

Gratitude requires a kind of deep courage. It's a choice we can make not only for ourselves, but as a way to connect with everyone else. That's where the beauty lies—in the sense of connection that, in the end, sustains us.

—Jack Kornfield, interview in *Body & Soul*

Brenda

When I'm teaching at a writing conference or an intensive writing workshop, I try to find time to lead my students in a guided relaxation centered around images of gratitude. I want to do this because I know how much stress they're under, and I know how stress can get in the way even as it pushes us to go further. This little meditation, for me, is one of the best teachings I can offer—for writing and for the writing life.

So I have those who are willing gather in a classroom; I ask them to lie down, an unaccustomed posture within these institutional walls, so already our relationship to ourselves and our learning begins to shift. We begin with three deep inhalations, expanding the belly, and then let the breath out in an audible sigh. We feel the ground supporting us, and with that support we start to travel through our bodies, the breath touching every part—the top of the head, the eyelids, the mouth, the neck, the shoulders, the spine—and allow each part to give a little, to yield its habitual control.

The room grows still then, and the quiet runs deep. Even the rhythmic snores of several people feels like an organic part of the silence, rather than a disturbance.

If I feel the group is ready and open to it, I ask the participants to become aware of their hearts, to touch their hearts with their breath. I ask them to give a little bow to their hearts, that small organ that works ceaselessly to keep us alive. I ask them to give a little bow to their lungs. We move our awareness like this through the deep recesses of our bodies, stopping to give little imperceptible nods of gratitude to every organ, every little neglected part—our elbows, our wrists, our knees.

Even if our bodies give us trouble, we can still forgive them. We tap into the vast store of gratitude and compassion that can be revived through this little bit of attention. And when our bodies become quiet, the mind takes on a welcoming quality that allows whatever will enter to enter. I'm thinking of Rumi's famous poem "The Guest House":

> This being human is a guest house.
> Every morning a new arrival.
>
> A joy, a depression, a meanness,
> some momentary awareness comes
> as an unexpected visitor.
>
> Welcome and entertain them all!
> Even if they're a crowd of sorrows,
> who violently sweep your house
> empty of its furniture,

still, treat each guest honorably.
He may be clearing you out
for some new delight.

The dark thought, the shame, the malice,
meet them at the door laughing,
and invite them in.

Be grateful for whoever comes,
because each has been sent
as a guide from beyond.

In this poem, the self becomes a clean slate, an empty place, grateful for the myriad "guests" that are bound to arrive. The poem speaks of being in a perpetual stance of *welcome*.

At the end of the guided meditation, when I bring the students out of this deeply relaxed state, they all look much different: Their faces are soft, open, glowing. They move slowly. We don't say much after this; I send them back out to do their writing, ideally with a little more space in which to find their voices, their words.

In the mindfulness tradition, gratitude often takes the form of bowing. We bow when we enter and leave the meditation hall; we bow to our cushions and to each other; we bow to our food before we eat. All this bowing can be confusing or off-putting to newcomers, and sometimes we ask them to think of it as a form of stretching until they get used to it. We say, "When in doubt, bow." It can't hurt.

I think when we take on the posture of gratitude, of bowing to ourselves and the world, we take at least one step toward getting out of our own way. This posture of bowing, of submission, can be difficult for Westerners. We must struggle against our instinct to be upright, to be beholden or submissive to no one, and instead surrender our egos, literally drop to the ground. But once we get the hang of it, we realize the pleasure of letting go of this solid, proud, individual self. We begin to see bowing as the only response in the face of the world's beauty, and its challenges. Saying thank you to whatever arises.

I've made it a habit lately to give an imperceptible bow—sometimes only in my mind—just before entering any situation that I anticipate will be difficult. The change in my attitude is subtle but profound; rather than resisting difficulties, I'm in a posture to embrace them and perhaps, sometimes, find my way more gracefully than I might have otherwise.

One of my favorite poems by W. S. Merwin, "Thanks," shows this posture so clearly. While enumerating the harsh realities of a modern world, the speaker keeps saying thank you, even in the midst of the worst:

> Listen
> with the night falling we are saying thank you
> we are stopping on the bridge to bow from the railings
> we are running out of the glass rooms
> with our mouths full of food to look at the sky
> and say thank you
> we are standing by the water thanking it
> standing by the window looking out
> in our directions. . . .
>
> over telephones we are saying thank you
> in doorways and in the backs of cars and in elevators
> remembering wars and the police at the door

and the beatings on stairs we are saying thank you
in the banks we are saying thank you
in the faces of the officials and the rich
and of all who will never change
we go on saying thank you thank you

with the animals dying around us
taking our feelings we are saying thank you
with the forests falling faster than the minutes
of our lives we are saying thank you
with the words going out like cells of a brain
with the cities growing over us
we are saying thank you faster and faster
with nobody listening we are saying thank you
we are saying thank you and waving
dark though it is

Though the picture Merwin paints is a bleak one, the narrator at the center of it all still bows and says thank you. While some take his tone as accusatory—accusing us of submitting to indignities and horrors without taking action to stop them—I've always read the poem as a testament to the power of retaining a mindful presence in the midst of suffering. By saying thank you, we are actually *more* powerful, capable of great action. Suffering happens every minute, and every minute we choose how to respond.

It's easy to be grateful for what we perceive as beautiful; more challenging is to be truly grateful for what is usually taken as ugly or dangerous. All of it is part of being alive, and all of it is fodder for strong writing.

Holly

I'm looking out the window of our hotel in San Diego at an ocean pockmarked by rain. Rain runs down the windows in rivulets, puddles on the roof of the building below us, splashes onto the sidewalk where a small figure hurries past, head tucked under a newspaper. John and I are here in San Diego to have Thanksgiving with his family. We drove down the long stretch of coastline from the Bay Area over the last two days, all the while imagining burying our toes in the white sand of one of the many beaches that stretch along the coast. But it's rained most of the last two days, rained as we drove the harrowing maze of freeways that interweave through LA like a circulatory system, rained as we drove down the Pacific Highway, stopping briefly in San Clemente for lunch at Pedro's Tacos.

We are here for family, not for sun, I find myself repeating. But I can hear the querulous voice of my child self surfacing, the self that felt personally injured every time it rained on vacation, or on the summer days I wanted to spend at the beach with friends.

This, then, has become my practice: to accept that I can't control the weather, that no amount of wishing will make the rain stop, the clouds part, the sun break through. And how ironic to be reminded of this on Thanksgiving, the day for giving thanks for all that we have. So today I am practicing gratitude for this rain, here, where it is so desperately needed. For rain falling in the desert to the east—Anza-Borrego—rain that will seep into the earth, cause cacti to bloom that haven't bloomed in months, rain that will form pools in the gutters for the pigeons, which will immerse their iridescent feathers, shaking the water droplets loose. Rain falling on the too many SUVs on the freeway, driving too fast to Thanksgiving dinner this afternoon. Rain falling as we all travel so that we may gather together with our imperfect lives to share imperfect food with our imperfect families, to give thanks for what we have.

Imperfect because when else are we so viscerally reminded of our human failings as when we gather with our families, whether related by blood or relationship? How many of us have sat down to holiday meals at which, despite everyone's best intentions, the conversation veers into dangerous territory? So I remind myself to enlarge my practice to be grateful for my family, though we may or may not get along, and for the food we might not prepare or eat at home, in addition to this weather that will never yield to my wishes.

Soon we will join John's sister's family and her two neighbors on the back patio, surrounded by blooming scarlet bougainvillea for Thanksgiving dinner, each of us bringing what makes this day special; for one it will be ham, for another a spinach soufflé, for another glazed carrots. We will set the table, arrange the flowers, consult on the turkey, stir flour into the gravy. We will want everything to be perfect: the turkey not dry, gravy not lumpy, carrots not mushy. We will want everyone to get along.

Of course, because the world is imperfect, this doesn't happen—and we will be reminded again of the imperfection of love.

Now we are flying home where we will gather for our annual post-Thanksgiving feast with friends who, over the years, have become our Northwest family. We will drink local wine, eat salmon and smoked tuna from local fishermen, yams and arugula from local farmers. On the way there, we will stop at Finnriver Farm to participate in their annual Thanking the Ground celebration, which seems exactly right at the end of a good harvest season. Since we may not all celebrate traditional Thanksgiving, this ceremony offers another way to express what's at the heart of the thanksgiving ritual: gratitude to the earth and the food that sustains us. As we fly home, I'm grateful to live in the Northwest, for the community that feeds me, for all our imperfect selves as we try to remember to want whatever is on our table, whatever lies before us.

Contemplation Practices

1. Make a list of all the things you are grateful for in your life—big or small—and post it where you will see it frequently. Sharon Salzberg, co-founder of the Insight Meditation Society, says, "It often takes conscious effort [to be grateful]. . . . Sometimes we have to be adventurous about it, to pay attention and look at things from a new angle. . . .When you can stop and look around and see what's right, it will fill you with gratitude, and bring with it a kind of joy." Observe your state of mind—does anything change after a few weeks of practicing gratitude?

2. Make a list of some things you can't change, then spend a few minutes meditating on each one, accepting and being grateful for it. Then make a list of the things you can change, choosing one to focus on over the next week.

3. Consider spending one day doing a practice of "bowing" (even if it's an imperceptible bow, done only in your mind) as you move through the different areas of your life. Bow before you enter a meeting. Bow before you eat your lunch at your desk. Bow before you give your child a bath. See if anything changes in your perception.

Writing Practices

1. Using W. S. Merwin's "Thanks" as a model, write a list poem or a short prose piece that conveys what you can say "thank you" to, whether it be beautiful or not so beautiful. Try to capture Merwin's sense of breathless urgency in the rhythms of your sentences or lines.

2. In the prologue to his memoir *Planet of the Blind*, Stephen Kuusisto describes being lost in Grand Central Station with his guide dog, Corky:

> We wash through the immense vault with no idea about how to find our train or the information kiosk. And just now it doesn't matter. None of the turmoil or anxiety of being lost will reach us because moving is holy, the very motion is a breeze from Jerusalem. This blindness of mine still allows me to see colors and shapes that seem windblown; the great terminal is supremely lovely in its swaying hemlock darknesses and sudden pools of rose-colored electric light. We don't know where we are, and though the world is dangerous, it's also haunting in its beauty. Even to a lost man with a speck of something like seeing, this minute here, just standing, taking in the air as a living circus, this is what tears of joy are for.

Using this passage as a model, write a scene of a small moment in time when you felt inexplicably grateful. Try to choose a circumstance that one wouldn't expect to feel grateful for. Use all your senses to convey this moment.

3. Write an imitation of Rumi's "The Guest House." Start with the line "This being human is a _____" and come up with your own metaphor for being human that acknowledges or welcomes imperfection. Try to follow his playful rhythm.

Twelve

Travel as Contemplative Practice

If our lives are dominated by a search for happiness, then perhaps few activities reveal as much about the dynamics of this quest—all its ardor and paradoxes—than our travels. They express, however inarticulately, an understanding of what life might be about outside of the constraints of work and of the struggle for survival.

—Alain de Botton, *The Art of Travel*

Brenda

I'm at Kabuki Hot Springs in San Francisco with my old friend Rhea, sitting in the dim recesses of a huge sauna in a Japanese spa. I left my glasses on the bench outside, so everything's softened, blurred. There's gentle flute music wafting in at just the right volume through invisible speakers. I sit back against the heated wood slats, my body warming, sweat just beginning to prick at the edges of my pores. There are women here of all shapes and sizes and ages, and we're all quietly settling down together, the worries and stresses of the world sloughing off. I feel a simple peace infusing my entire body: a peace that does not feel labored or hard-won but just there, a pool of stillness in the midst of women stripped down to their bare selves.

And since I'm away from my normal routines—since I'm traveling in a place that is both familiar to me and exotic—I feel alert, awake, even in the midst of this elaborate relaxation ritual. Travel can be another form of "active contemplation." We can see our travels as one giant walking meditation, our senses heightened, paying attention in a sharper way (even without our glasses!).

After we leave this beautiful spa, Rhea and I will be thrust back into the sharp hum of city life—ringing trolley cars, busy sidewalks, bakeries with their wares displayed so enticingly. We'll ride a Muni train so crowded we have to literally elbow our way out. Rhea's a wonderful travel guide since she lived here years ago, so I follow her through the city, into and out of busses and trams, down to Golden Gate Park and up Telegraph Hill. And maybe it's because I'm with such a good friend, or maybe it's the after-effects of the spa, but I sense little islands of quiet within myself, even in the midst of this vibrant, chaotic city.

We go inside the "Giant Camera" behind the Cliff House; we're the only ones inside the small, darkened room, where you can see—on a giant spinning disc—the outside world projected in through the simple action of mirrors and light. We stand there a long time in the quiet, watching it all revolve, as if we've stumbled upon the hub of the world.

When I look back on it, so much of my "spiritual" writing has sprung from travel, whether it's an excursion to a city like San Francisco, a camping trip, or a solo journey through Portugal. In one of my first essays, "Basha Leah," my contemplation of Catholic saints in Portuguese shrines led me to consider my own experience with prayer, my Jewish upbringing, and the many ways I have sought my own forms of communion. It begins with simple observations:

> In Portugal I walk slowly, like the old Portuguese men: hands crossed
> behind my back, head tilted forward, lips moving soundlessly around

a few simple words. This posture comes naturally in a country wedded to patience, where the bark of the cork oak takes seven years to mature, and olives swell imperceptibly within their leaves. Food simmers a long time—kid stew, bread soup, roast lamb. Celtic dolmens rise slab-layered in fields hazy with lupine. . . .

A few days ago, in a sixteenth-century church in Évora, I entered the Chapel of the Bones. Skulls and ribs and femurs mortared the walls, the bones of five thousand monks arranged in tangled, overlapping tiers. A yellow light bulb burned in the dank ceiling. Two mummified corpses flanked the altar. A placard above the lintel read: *Nos ossos que aqui estamos, Pelos vossos esperamos.* "We bones here are waiting for yours. . . ." Visitors murmured all around me, but not in prayer; none of us knelt in front of that dark shrine. What kind of prayer, I wondered, does a person say in the presence of so many bodies, jumbled into mosaic, with no prospect of an orderly resurrection? A prayer of terror, I imagined, or an exclamation of baffled apology.

When I began writing this piece, I had no idea where it would go. I had to trust in the power of contemplative observation and the faithful rendering of detail to lead me somewhere significant. I jotted down notes in a travel journal so I wouldn't forget these details, and in my first versions of this essay I was simply trying to re-create my experience of Portugal on the page. But such transcriptions can fall flat—boring for both reader and writer—unless the details lead you to something deeper, some theme that has resonance.

In this case, as I touched again the details of that Portuguese landscape and its underground shrine, the word *prayer* arose as a beacon, and the essay took on new depth and direction. Now I had a sense of what scenes to include from that trip (and, perhaps more importantly, what to exclude). Parallel threads—my upbringing as a Jewish girl; my yoga practice; esoteric facts about Judaism; my mother's hysterectomy—began to weave through this primary narrative to give it new texture and meaning.

My quest in Portugal—at least in this particular essay—is fueled by questions. *Quest*, after all, springs from *question*, and in contemplative travel writing, the questions spur us most deeply—not the answers. In this case, I found myself deeply involved in the question of how to pray. While there are no definitive answers to this inquiry, my journey was enlivened by the search for them.

Sometimes we can also act as travelers in our familiar landscapes, seeing them anew, if we practice paying attention. For example, I live in one of the most beautiful places in the Northwest, a destination for both tourists and retirees. There's a walk my dog, Abbe, and I take at least once a week along the bay, and if I'm immersed in my brain babble I barely notice where I am. But if I stop for even a moment and look up—if I pretend I'm a tourist in my own town—I notice again the outline of the San Juan Islands on the horizon, and closer up the bright purple starfish clinging to the rocks at low tide. I notice the coffeehouse with its comfortable chairs overlooking the water. I notice the balancing rock sculptures that an anonymous artist has built along the shore. I often exclaim, if only to myself, "Look where we are!"

In Rebecca McClanahan's essay "Signs and Wonders," a habitual stroll through Central Park in Manhattan becomes its own kind of pilgrimage. She sets off on a walk through the park with a question in mind: She needs to decide whether to renew the lease on the sublet she and her husband have been renting for the past four years. As with any good quest, this walk is spurred by a question, and this question informs everything she sees:

> Maybe it's the wrong day to decide. Maybe I need some air. Maybe I need a sign. So I go where I always go when I need a sign—the park,

and oh look, a day so beautiful you'd gladly pay the universe if it were charging. The leaves on the ginkgos are falling as I speak, gold coins upon gold coins. And there in the pond are my geese, my ducks, how I admire them. Look, one is passing up bread crumbs to catch a blossom. He's eating flowers.

As she walks in the park, McClanahan notices everything, searching for a sign. So even the most mundane and unlovely things take on luster. She talks with a disabled artist on a park bench, encounters a homeless man in a familiar gazebo. She passes many literal signs on this walk, including a rule for fishing in the pond: "Catch and Release." This small detail becomes the driving force of the essay:

Yes, that's it. Catch and release. . . . Enjoy for the moment, then let it go—the fiery carp, the brilliant day, the black-eyed children with the dimpled hands, the coins on the ginkgo trees swirling down, down. Our lives are sublets anyway, and too quickly gone at that. And what better place to live out our leases.

In his book *The Art of Travel,* Alain de Botton writes, "We can see beauty well enough just by opening our eyes, but how long this beauty will survive in memory depends on how intentionally we have apprehended it." Taking on the mantle of the tourist, even in our home territory, restores our intentionality. We can do a walking meditation at a fast pace, paying attention, every step leading us to new vistas.

Holly

As a teacher and writer, I frequently travel to unfamiliar cities for conferences and readings, and while I enjoy the change of pace, the stimulation can feel a bit overwhelming. Over the years, I've learned I need to pack—along with my toothbrush—the practices that will keep me centered: my CD of the monks and nuns of Deer Park Monastery chanting for twenty minutes of morning meditation, my yoga mat so I can stretch in whatever space I can find. When I have a break, I seek out a community swimming pool or walking trails. Instead of staying in the conference hotels, I stay in B & Bs. I use public transit, and I try to visit a museum or two. In order to keep from mindlessly eating too much sugar, I carry nuts, fruit, and a stash of good dark chocolate. I try to remember to write every day in my journal, even if it's just notes for a morning poem. I've learned that when I do these things, I'm able to find that island of calm—the hub in the midst of the spinning world that Brenda wrote about—and can better enjoy all that an unfamiliar city has to offer.

Usually, though, my chosen travels take me away from cities. When summer comes, if I'm not in Alaska, I like to hit the open road with my partner, John, and Fox, getting to know new terrain. In fact, right now we've just left I-5 and are winding through the wine country of northern California on a two-lane road, slowing down at each small town, then gaining elevation, curving up into the filtered light of the oak forest. The late afternoon sun lights up the dry grasses of the hillsides just as I slip in my favorite Kate Wolf CD, and she begins to sing about the "rolling golden hills of California."

John grew up in these hills; this is his home range, his native ground. As a Minnesota transplant to the Northwest, my home range is woven of water, trees, and, more recently, mountains—a far cry from this landscape, though I'm slowly growing to love it, too. Can we love more than one place? John and I wonder aloud, as the rental car weaves around another curve in the golden hills, dusk falling, a red-tailed hawk soaring through the wide branches of an oak.

The next day I wake early, still thinking about our conversation, dress in the dark, and hike up to a teahouse, a meditation hut on the side of one of the golden hills that looks out over the valley. From there, I can watch the gold wafer of sun roll up over the next hilltop and think about what connects us so viscerally to a place—and how it is that we can love more than one. As I sit in the teahouse, I remember to turn my focus closer and then notice all the offerings —feathers, stones, a wooden deer, Indonesian coins—left on the altar. I'm reminded how paying attention helps to ground us in a new place.

When we're in unfamiliar terrain, we can't help but notice everything as we try to gain familiarity, an ease with our new world. John and I visit this retreat center as often as we can, whenever we're driving down to visit his family. As I've climbed this trail over the years, I've come to know the manzanita by the feel of its peeling bark, the eucalyptus by its pungent smell. I look for the perfect cups of acorns, fallen from the oaks, lining the paths. I listen for the hooves of the mule deer that also use this trail to traverse the hillside. It's an intimacy that grows with time, as with all relationships. As Georgia O'Keefe once said, "It takes time to see a flower, to really see it"; she couldn't have painted her bold, sensuous paintings of flowers if she hadn't first *really* seen them. I remind myself to look up the oaks in my field guide when I return; just as we need to really see the wild creatures, we also establish intimacy when we can call them by name.

How will we know this intimacy if we don't turn off the highway onto the back roads, aren't willing to get to know the inhabitants—human, animal, vegetal—of a new place? This is how we come to know our home ground, whether this is where we once chose to put down roots or a new home we want to embrace.

Can we have more than one home ground? We can, but we have to earn that right. I can't yet call northern California my home ground—I need to live here through the seasons, become more intimate with all the inhabitants, human and wild. But I can enjoy the pleasure of getting to know a new place if I keep my senses open, take careful note of what's around me. When I do, I'll learn not only that the acorns come from *Quercus kelloggii*, the California black oak, I'll deepen my connection to—and appreciation for—these rolling hills that I could so easily speed past on the freeway, intent on our final destination.

As Brenda points out, there are many ways to travel. Traveling can simply represent a receptive state of mind, an openness to new experience, or what the Buddhists call "beginner's mind." While the word *beginner* can have a negative connotation, in this usage it reminds us to approach all our experiences with the enthusiasm, innocence, and fresh eyes of a beginner. We all remember the giddy exhilaration of riding a two-wheeler bike for the first time, or the anticipation laced with trepidation of slurping our first raw oyster. Now, when I catch myself becoming jaded or just not appreciating where I am, I remind myself to be a beginner. And because traveling in unfamiliar places makes us, literally, beginners again, traveling, too, reminds us to be open.

I've traveled to the same stretch of Alaskan coastline for thirty seasons now, but each time I come back, I become a beginner again. I'm reminded that it may take days of quiet on the water or hiking in the old-growth forest to feel part of the landscape I love. I spent many seasons working on fishing boats, with the steady thrum of the diesel engine separating me from the land and water, looking forward to the moment when we'd finally drop the anchor, shut down the engine, and let the sounds, sights, and smells of the world flood back in.

My travels, like the salmon's, take me north, not to the cobbled streets of ancient cities but to the cobbles and rills of streams, the muskeg aroma of an ancient rainforest, the Tongass National Forest. While I hope to someday again stand in the Parthenon as the full moon rises, get lost in the many rooms of the British Museum, I also dream of trekking in the Himalayas, of kayaking above the Arctic Circle. For me, travel isn't just about experiencing the diversity of human life in cities but a way of exploring the diversity of our natural ecosystems.

As Sven Lindblad, the founder of Lindblad Expeditions, said, "True travel is about how you've enriched your lives through encounters with beauty, wildness and the seldom-seen." Of course, there are many ways we can do this—not just on expensive eco-trips but on backpacking and camping trips in our own state and in national parks. What matters is the attentiveness we bring with us—our willingness to watch and listen carefully, the curiosity of beginner's mind we remind ourselves to pack, along with bug spray.

Years after I'd left fishing, I was lucky to work with a fellow former fisherman, Kurt Hoelting, on one of his Inside Passages trips, which combine meditation with kayaking. We spent ten days kayaking in silence, eating our meals in silence, talking only briefly in the evenings or to point out the white head of a bald eagle in a tall Sitka spruce, giving each other the gift of being able to be fully present with whatever the day offered: a fleeting glimpse of a seal, the screech of an eagle, a pair of humpback whales feeding in the tide rip.

Because I'm usually working on boats as the skipper or naturalist, I can't always experience Alaska in this way, but I'm grateful for whatever quiet moments I can find, early morning when the sea shimmers in oyster light and I can't tell which is real—us or our reflection shimmering back. One season, I spent a week with Kurt and Dan, another former fisherman, on Dan's boat exploring the west coast of Chichagof Island. The trip was Dan's idea: We'd combine our love of Alaska with our practice of meditation, Dan's interest in photography and film, Kurt's and my love of writing—and see what happened. One morning, after meditating together on the front deck as the fog lifted, I made a few notes in my journal, an entry that eventually became part of a short essay called "Hidden":

When we arrived at our first night's anchorage inside Piehle Passage, the steep, rocky coast was shrouded in fog. In the morning, the fog lifted like a woman raising her skirt, sun shimmering on glacier-scarred flanks. Even the granite cliffs seemed to tremble. What was revealed seemed sacred. No boats were visible, no floatplanes, no sight or sound of human life. We kayaked in silence, walked the beach in silence, letting the land reveal only what she chose. . . .

The Alaska I love dwells where it eludes me, where words fail, shutters freeze. Not the white mountains, distant and austere, not the calving ice dropping theatrically into the sea. Instead, the interstices where impossibly blue ice begins to melt. *Quieter. Slower.* The *shush* and burble of the tide inching back into the estuary across long mud flats. Starfish the color of eggplant, of pumpkins. Slick drifts of bladderwrack, undulant snakes of bull kelp. A bear loping alone up the beach, tracks erased by the next tide. Raven's hollow water drop call. White femur of a deer lying still in waving green grasses, bear scat shot through with huckleberries. Scrim of frost on aspen leaves.

The Alaska landscape so dramatic, it's taken many seasons to see what's hidden, to be grateful for what I don't see as well as what I do. Last summer, I spent almost an hour watching a slug tilt its strange head down to drink from a still pool. The intimacy of this simple act stunned me. How is it that I'd never paused long enough to notice the erotic unfurling of its antennae, its small mouth slit open and begin to sip?

Even though I'd watched fog lift countless times, had traveled past steep granite cliffs in many boats, it wasn't until I could slow down—through our shared contemplative practice—that I felt connected to the landscape in an intimate way, could feel the granite cliffs tremble, could know the spirit of the place I love as something alive, even erotic.

Whether we're returning to familiar home ground or discovering new home ground, there's always more to know when we train ourselves to observe the smallest details, to listen deeply. By seeing with the eyes of the traveler, observing closely even the landscapes and neighborhoods that we think we know well, we can practice "beginner's mind." When we do, we might discover something new, not just about our neighborhoods but about ourselves. And when we do, we have more rich details to bring to our writing.

Contemplation Practices

1. The next time you travel, even if it's somewhere local, try to remember to stop and breathe, to practice walking meditation, even if it's just for a few minutes. Write down random observations and details, even if you don't know why those details are sticking with you, and use them to start new pieces when you get home.

2. The next time you visit a new place, reflect on both what's familiar and what's not. Take advantage of being in new country by seeing how much you can notice about it: the new sights, sounds, and—especially—smells. Remind yourself that this, too, is your home, even if it's not your familiar home. Consult a field guide so you can be on a first-name basis with the inhabitants—whether trees, plants, or animals.

3. If you enjoy sketching, try keeping an illustrated journal. Combine drawing with writing as a way to more fully experience—and record—what you see for future writing.

4. The next time you're packing for a business or family trip to an unfamiliar city, make a list of the things you need to bring with you to feel centered—a favorite relaxation tape, your workout clothes, some good dark chocolate. Download a map of the neighborhood near your hotel and look for walking trails, museums, or other places you can visit that will allow you to get to know the city itself. Make a commitment to visit one of them each day.

Writing Practices

1. If you have a travel journal from a trip, go back and see what particular "questions" you can distill from some of the details you chose to record. It may seem as though we are recording images and memories at random, but in reality there are hundreds of things we are noticing all the time, especially when we are traveling; what we choose to remember usually has some personal significance. Once you have a question in mind, see if there are parallel threads you can write that use the travel narrative as a type of container for this question.

2. Think about a trip you took and write down a list of images that stay with you. Use a repeating refrain, such as "I noticed . . ." or "I would like to see again . . ." to keep the list going. See if there are any surprises in what comes to mind. What stays with you and why?

3. Take a walk with a deliberate question in mind. Make it a "quest": What new details can you discover in this familiar landscape? How can you be a traveler in your own neighborhood?

4. Write about an unfamiliar landscape or place. Look up the names of three trees or plants you don't already know and include them in the piece. You can write this as a fictional story, nonfiction essay, or a poem. What matters is that your research will help you come to know the new place and add credible details to your writing.

Thirteen

Encounters with the Wild

> . . . What I want happens
> not when the deer freezes in the shade
> and looks at you and you hold very still
> and meet her gaze but in the moment after
> when she flicks her ears & starts to feed again.
>
> —Robert Hass, "Santa Lucia"

Brenda

I once saw a pod of orca whales off the shore at Lime Kiln Park on San Juan Island. I was traveling with my younger brother and his two daughters, and we had stopped at the park renowned as the best place to see whales. "Now don't get your hopes up," I said, as we walked down a trail glowing with dozens of madrone trees. We got to the observation site, with its low cinderblock walls holding interpretive signs that would teach us everything we needed to know about a whale—if we saw one.

Haro Strait sparkled before us, the water calm. We shaded our eyes to look in every direction, peered through the binoculars. Nothing. The water seemed mysterious, coy. The girls got restless, and so I walked with the oldest, Ali, up to the lighthouse, where a whiteboard declared that the last whale sighting had been two days earlier. "Oh, well," I shrugged, and Ali picked up a few stones, skipped them across the bluff.

As we walked back, I saw my brother frantically waving his arms, and we began to run. There, to the south, we could see the backs of whales and an occasional spout. We looked through the binoculars, passing them from hand to hand, and then we didn't need the binoculars anymore because the animals were just a few feet offshore, doing everything the interpretive signs told us they might do: spy-hopping, breaching, leaping through the air, rolling in twists that looked like delight incarnate. At one point, a group of three kayakers came into view around the bend, and we saw them stop short, pointing with their paddles. Five of the whales lined up in front of them, dove, and came up on the other side, to the cheers and whoops of all us onlookers. The kayakers looked stunned and ecstatic.

On shore, we were ecstatic, too. My brother and I hugged, I hugged my nieces, and we would have hugged the strangers around us if decorum had not taken over. "I can't believe it," we said over and over. I've never seen whales there again (though I've stopped there many, many times), and so the memory of that one encounter makes for an even stronger connection with my brother and nieces. We've shared in something extraordinary. And we stayed there long enough, were patient enough, to see it.

In her poem "The Moose," Elizabeth Bishop gets at this sense of shared connection forged by witnessing a wild animal. It's a long poem, written in Bishop's observational voice, much of it evoking the lulling bus ride through the Nova Scotia landscape, the murmurings of the passengers as they come aboard, the small details the speaker sees in passing—such as the fog settling "in the white hens' feathers, / in gray glazed cabbages." She sees "the sweet peas cling / to their wet white string / on the whitewashed fences." Then the bus grinds to a halt and all the passengers crowd to the windows.

A moose has come out of
the impenetrable wood
and stands there, looms, rather,
in the middle of the road.
It approaches; it sniffs at
the bus's hot hood. . . .

Some of the passengers
exclaim in whispers,
childishly, softly,
"Sure are big creatures."
"It's awful plain."
"Look! It's a she!"

Taking her time,
she looks the bus over,
grand, otherworldly.
Why, why do we feel
(we all feel) this sweet
sensation of joy?

The animal is both of that landscape and apart from it, a sudden apparition. Bishop is moved to ask herself a question, the same one I ask of myself. I don't have an answer; perhaps there isn't one. "Why, why do we feel / (we all feel) this sweet / sensation of joy?" She puts that phrase in parentheses, "(we all feel)," like a whisper, a secret. Perhaps—like all such transformative moments—all we can do is experience it. We can't really know the reason we feel such joy, we can only feel it.

However, sometimes writing about an encounter with a wild animal can take a more somber turn. The animal's presence can help us articulate grief or pain that we haven't yet been able to describe directly. For example, in her beautiful short essay "The Sloth," Jill Christman describes encountering a sloth in Costa Rica, just as she is mourning the death of her fiancé:

> Later, standing under a trickle of water in the wooden outdoor shower, I heard a rustle, almost soundless, and looking up, expecting something small, I saw my first three-toed sloth. Mottled and filthy, he hung by his meat-hook claws not five feet above my head in the cecropia tree. He peered down at me, his flattened head turned backwards on his neck. Here is a fact: a sloth cannot regulate the temperature of his blood. He must live near the equator.
>
> I thought I knew slow, but this guy, this guy was *slow*.

As she contemplates the sloth and its interminable crawl across the tree branch, Christman is able to finally acknowledge the "slowness" of her own grief, the way her pain has anesthetized her. "Dripping and naked in the jungle," she writes, "I thought, *That sloth is as slow as grief.* We were numb to the speed of the world. We were one temperature." The sloth and the narrator now come together as "we," and Christman is able, in a short amount of time, to express a deep truth in a startling way.

In "Some Notes on the Gazer Within," the poet Larry Levis says, "Animals are objects of contemplation, but they are also, unlike us, without speech, without language, except in their own instinctual systems. When animals occur in poems, then, I believe they are often emblems for the muteness of the poet, for what he or she cannot express." The animal can act as a mirror and a witness, helping us speak what is unspeakable.

Holly

Brenda's story of seeing the pod of orcas reminds me of my first encounter with whales. Even though it was more than thirty years ago, I can still remember the first time I saw a humpback whale; I can even still smell the whale's krill-laced breath. It's my first trip as deckhand on Peter Shugren's tender *Cypress* and we're running back to Petersberg through Frederick Sound, the hold sloshing with sixty thousand pounds of Taku cohos in refrigerated seawater. When we reach Five-Finger Lighthouse, Peter sees a few spouts off to the west. He hands the heavy black binoculars to me, says, "Take a look about two o'clock, slightly off our starboard bow, you'll see a whale feeding." I peer through the glasses, focusing until a glistening black back surfaces—just barely—above the water, blows once, then slowly sinks back down. The spout hangs in the air, iridescent, a zillion diamonds. I turn to Peter. "Can we get closer?"

"We'll give it a try," he says. We turn and run parallel to where she's feeding in the tide rip. When we're within a half mile, Peter throttles back the engine, then shuts it down. "We'll let her decide if she wants to come visit," he says. He puts on Mozart and we both go out on deck, sit on the heavy black wood rail, listening to the music and watching as the whale slowly works her way up the tide rip, breathing steadily, one *chuff* after another, seemingly oblivious to our presence as she gets closer. Then she's right next to us, her massive gray body extending the length of the sixty-five-foot *Cypress*, then she's rolling on her side to gaze up at us with a round eye bigger than a dinner plate. I can't speak, I can't even breathe. Then she slowly arches her rubbery back and dives, flukes hanging in the air, dripping, for what seems like forever, then vanishes, the sea smooth as if it had never happened. Ecstatic, I'm hugging Peter, thanking him, thanking the whale, thanking Mozart, brimming with gratitude and awe that can't be contained in my body or even on a sixty-five-foot boat. I pace the deck for hours that night, promising I'll be back.

I kept that promise, and I've now seen more humpback whales than I can count. I've spent the last ten seasons working as a naturalist, most recently on a beautiful fifty-two-foot wood boat, the *Gravina*. Of course, all the passengers want to see whales, but because they are wild, sometimes we see them and sometimes we don't. But once I learned to counter the passengers' expectation that I could produce whales on demand, I learned to appreciate—and encourage others to do the same—the whales' unpredictability as a critical aspect of their wildness.

In fact, I've learned that the whales seem to have a sixth sense about this; they often show up just when you've given up, turned the boat around. I don't know how many times I've gone out on the back deck for one last look and seen a whale breach right behind us. (They also have a great sense of humor: one year on the cruise ship, we were in the theater watching a video of humpback whales while outside, they circled the ship.) But when we are lucky enough to see them, to slow down and observe them as I did so many years ago on the *Cypress*, they always elicit that "sweet sensation of joy" that Elizabeth Bishop describes.

Such joy is revealed whenever we observe closely. Diane Ackerman writes in *The Moon by Whale Light*, "Each of the animals I write about I find beguiling in and of itself, but in all honesty, there is no animal that isn't fascinating if viewed up close and in detail." A good example of this perspective occurs in Lucia Perillo's poem "Dressage." She zooms in to view "up close and in detail" a horse in its pasture, and this observation stimulates an unexpected joy. The poem begins: "It was too good, too good / the white horse dancing in the field." She and her companion had stopped to observe the horse in its pasture and found the animal, unexpectedly, dancing. She goes on:

Too good the white horse, too good
the sad frogs telling stories in the valley,
too good the heron unfolding awkward
prehistoric wings, then lifting itself
against such doubt, such questionable odds.
And what about the cowbirds gathering
over the marsh at dusk in such numbers
they make the sky black, a spectacle
so close to holy that it leaves me dumb.

The horse leads the speaker to widen her vision to the multitude of life going on around her: the frogs, the heron, the cowbirds—they all now seem part of a sacred choreography that includes the poet. This encounter—a moment suspended in time, observed in specific detail—leads Perillo to a cry of gratitude: *It is too good. It is too good*, an almost bodily communion, a joy so great it's practically unbearable.

Perillo's poem artfully connects the wild with the domestic: so many species in this world, a wild thread of kinship running through all of us. I'm reminded of an essay by Barbara Kingsolver called "Small Wonder," based on an incident reported in the news, just a sentence that I'd read, too: *After being missing for three days, a sixteen-month-old baby in Iran was found safe and slumbering in the den of a mother bear, who'd suckled him to keep him alive.* From this incident, Kingsolver wrote a compelling essay exploring the possibility of connecting with the nonhuman world. Think of all the stories we grew up with, of children living with wolves, Romulus and Remus, the *Jungle Book;* surely some of these were based on true incidents, like that of the lost toddler in Iran. Perhaps this is more common than we realize. Perhaps this is the connection we long for still.

In his essay, "Writers and the War Against Nature," Gary Snyder offers a possible explanation for this longing: "There is a tame and also a wild side to the human mind. The tame side, like the farmer's field, has been disciplined and cultivated to produce a desired yield. It is useful, but limited. The wild side is larger, deeper, more complex, and though it cannot be fully known, it can be explored. . . . It has landscapes and creatures within it that will surprise us; it can refresh and scare us; it reflects the larger truths of our ancient selves, both animal and spiritual." Here Snyder talks about animal and spiritual as if they form a dichotomy, while recognizing that both are truths. But isn't it interesting that the way to the spiritual is so often *through* animals? Perhaps as our civilized culture takes us further from our animal and spiritual selves, we need contact with wild animals more than ever to remind us of the need for both.

Sometimes seeing animals may not only remind us of the wild side of our minds, but connect us with our deeper, unseen selves. In "Three Foxes by the Edge of the Field at Twilight," Jane Hirshfield writes of an unexpected encounter that moved her to new awareness.

> One ran,
> her nose to the ground,
> a rusty shadow
> neither hunting nor playing.
>
> One stood; sat; lay down; stood again.
>
> One never moved,
> except to turn her head a little as we walked.
>
> Finally we drew too close,
> and they vanished.
> The woods took them back as if they had never been.

I wish I had thought to put my face to the grass.

But we kept walking,
speaking as strangers do when becoming friends.

There is more and more I tell no one,
strangers nor loves.
This slips into the heart
without hurry, as if it had never been.

And yet, among the trees, something has changed.

Something looks back from the trees,
and knows me for who I am.

Hirshfield's poem begins with observation of the foxes, then moves, as her poems often do, to reflect on what's in the speaker's heart: "There is more and more I tell no one, / strangers nor loves. / This slips into the heart / without hurry, as if it had never been." In this chance encounter with wildness, the speaker feels seen: "Something looks back from the trees, / and knows me for who I am."

Once, at a retreat center in California, I found myself suddenly, unexpectedly, surrounded by wild turkeys. Here's how I remember it: On my way back down the trail from the teahouse on top of a hill, I hear a rustle in the dry, curling oak leaves. I stop to listen. A deer? As I peer around one of the oak trees, I see a flock of wild turkeys, oblivious to my presence, parading single file up the trail. They are so close I can see the sun shining through their loose, red gaggles; I can even see the bright bead of their eyes. I can't tell if they see me as they stride deliberately past. Then I'm walking down the trail, turkeys on either side, turkeys in front and behind, as if I am one of them, as if we are, in fact, all one family.

Perhaps through our encounters with animals and wildness, whether sought or accidental, we can begin to expand our sense of family. In doing so, we not only experience Bishop's "sweet sensation of joy," we are reminded of our connections to these wild creatures, to each other, and to our wilder, unseen selves.

Contemplation Practices

1. Go to a natural area close to your home—it could be a park in the city, a vacant lot, your backyard—and pay attention to *all* the creatures you see, including the less charismatic ones, like the slugs.

2. Reflect on Gary Snyder's description of the mind as having both a tame and a wild side, the latter of which "reflects the larger truths of our ancient selves, both animal and spiritual." Consider how the "tame mind" might be limited and what larger truths the "wild mind" might offer. Consider how time with "wildness"—even if it's just a squirrel in your backyard—connects you with those larger truths.

3. Think about the stories you read as a child that involved humans living with animals. What did you learn about animals as a result? Look for examples of cross-species interaction today. Reflect on what we might learn from these.

Writing Practices

1. Using Robert Hass's line "What I want happens . . ." (from the epigraph at the beginning of this chapter), begin a poem or prose piece that shows what you most desire from animals or your relationship to animals.

2. Write a scene about being with family or friends at a time when you encountered a wild animal together. Concentrate on the physical details to lead to emotional insights.

3. Write about an encounter with an animal that changed how you thought about that creature. Use the example of Bishop's "The Moose" to guide you.

4. As Jill Christman did in "The Sloth," look outward to see if an animal encounter can help you express deep emotion that previously remained inarticulate. Try to pinpoint a small, specific moment in time, describe the animal, and use those physical details to make the leap into more emotional or spiritual terrain.

5. Write a poem or short prose piece based on Perillo's "Dressage." Start with the line "It was too good." What was too good? What encounter with an animal would make you exclaim such a thing?

6. If you have encountered a wild animal, write about it in a way that reveals both the landscape and something new about yourself, as Jane Hirshfield did in her poem "Three Foxes by the Edge of the Field at Twilight." Was there a way in which you felt more "seen" from the encounter? Begin with careful observation, then move into how this interaction affected you. Be sure to include the details that will allow the reader to visualize it, too.

Fourteen

Our Animal Companions

Animals hold us to what is present, to who we are at the time.
. . . Because they have the ability to read our involuntary tics
and scents, we're transparent to them and thus exposed—we're
finally ourselves.

—Gretel Ehrlich, *The Solace of Open Spaces*

Brenda

I'm in PetSmart, a little lost (as I often feel in this store). There are so many things one can buy, and I wonder if that means I *need* to buy them. Do I need doggie toothpaste? Ear disinfectant? A little raincoat? Rope toys, rubber toys, chew toys? My dog, Abbe, doesn't care what I buy; she's just overjoyed to be here, sniffing out every smell in every corner, rolling on her back for every dog and person who passes by.

In the previous chapter, Holly and I talked mainly about encounters with wild animals, but it is often our domestic animals, our pets, who lead us out into the world in their quiet and humble ways. Perhaps they let us touch our own animal selves a little bit, the self who isn't so overwhelmed with the minutiae of everyday life.

When I first saw Abbe's picture, she was a three-month-old rescue puppy, her thumbnail portrait one of hundreds on Petfinder.com. I knew it instantly: "That's my dog—I'd better go get her." An application, three interviews, and a thousand trips to PetSmart later, there I was with a new creature in my house— a seven-pound bundle of golden fur and eyes and ears. She made herself right at home, much to the dismay of my cat, Madrona.

I found I could watch this puppy for a long time, just taking in the way her fur fell in waves across her chest. Walks soon became more than just walks—they became an opportunity to follow Abbe's nose, her delight, and soon I knew I would hardly ever be able to take a walk without her; it just wouldn't feel right.

I wrote an essay a few weeks later which started with just a single moment that had stayed in my mind: the way Abbe's snout rested on my wrist as I petted her to sleep. It was a moment of physical connection that stirred something new in me, something I had never yet experienced:

> When I sit next to my dog, Abbe, just before she falls asleep, and I stroke her fine-boned head, she turns just enough so that her nose somehow nuzzles between my wrist and my sleeve. She breathes in some scent she's found there—perhaps the smell of my pulse. I keep my hand very still, on the top of her head, her nose glued to my wrist as she snuffles and sighs. The whole house goes quiet then, all of us just breathing: the couch and the cat, the vase and the tulips, the mirror and the broom. All of us just here, just now, in the trance of a dog who knows nothing, yet, but grace.

Writing down that image led to a long essay, "Blessing of the Animals," that allowed me to express all manner of connections I feel with my family and my community. It wasn't a conscious process, but the essay unfolded quite naturally from this tactile moment of connection.

Abigail Thomas knows this sense of canine connection well. In her book *A Three Dog Life*, she describes how her dogs kept her steady in the aftermath of her husband's serious brain injury:

If you were to look into our apartment in the late morning, or early afternoon, or toward suppertime, you might find us together sleeping. Of course a good rainy day is preferable, but even on sunny summer days, the dogs and I get into bed. Rosie dives under the quilt on my right, Harry on my left, and we jam ourselves together. After a little bit Harry starts to snore, Rosie rests her chin on my ankle, the blanket rises and falls with our breathing, and I feel only gratitude. We are doing something as necessary to our well-being as food or air or water. We are steeping ourselves, reassuring ourselves, renewing ourselves, three creatures of two species, finding comfort in the simple exchange of body warmth.

I love the way she allows me to peer through her window and glimpse this intimate moment between "two species." The details are the simple, common ones: a quilt, the snore of a dog, a chin on an ankle. It all comes back to the breath: "The blanket rises and falls with our breathing," and through the evocation of this simple scene, gratitude arises.

Abbe is now four years old, and I don't want to think of my household ever being without her. She's become my family, along with the cat, and I know myself at home only when their bodies anchor me in the bed. Sometimes I find myself wondering what she's thinking, what she would have to teach me as yet another master of contemplation. Mark Doty does this in his delightful poem "Golden Retrievals," told from the point of view of his dog Beau:

Fetch? Balls and sticks capture my attention
seconds at a time. Catch? I don't think so.
Bunny, tumbling leaf, a squirrel who's—oh
joy—actually scared. Sniff the wind, then

I'm off again: muck, pond, ditch, residue
of any thrillingly dead thing. And you?
Either you're sunk in the past, half our walk,
thinking of what you never can bring back,

or else you're off in some fog concerning
—tomorrow, is that what you call it? My work:
       to unsnare time's warp (and woof!), retrieving,
my haze-headed friend, you. This shining bark

a Zen master's bronzy gong, calls you here,
entirely, now: bow-wow, bow-wow, bow-wow.

Doesn't it just seem so true? An animal's delight in the present can wake us up, if we allow it. I hope we can always hear that "bow-wow, bow-wow, bow-wow" calling us home.

Holly

Six years ago, a skinny husky showed up in our yard. We called him the ghost dog, because he was just a shadow lurking in the bushes, afraid to come to us, even when we held out biscuits. Gradually, with encouragement from a neighbor dog, he finally came into the yard, grabbed a biscuit, and ran. It took another month before he'd come up to the front door, but soon he was showing up every day for his biscuit handout. He was clearly living on the streets—he was so thin that we could see every rib—and had mastered the fine art of tipping over garbage cans to forage for food.

He obviously needed a home and a steady meal ticket. Since I already had two cats who would never agree to a dog in the family, I began looking for a home for him. In the meantime, he acquired a name, Fox, his own food bowl, his own blue collar and leash. One summer day, as some friends and I sat under the shade of the wisteria, I said something about needing to find a home for Fox. My friends looked at each other, and then Melissa said: "Holly, Fox has already found his home." A few days later, I took him to the Kitsap Humane Society and formally adopted him.

Like any good dog owner, I enrolled Fox in an obedience class, but quickly realized the class was for me, not him. He's smart, catches on quickly, and can be obedient if it suits his needs. He was bored with—and slept through— the obedience class, but still managed to win runner-up as Most Obedient in the Indianola Days Pet Parade (losing out to a turtle). Finally, I came to understand that Fox was in fact training me. Fox taught me about the importance of daily walks, not just one but several: down to the beach, out to the church camp in the next bay, and back up the eighty-seven stairs from the beach. Fox is now part of the family, along with our two cats, who finally accepted his presence.

Fox and the cats are connected in another way, too: All of them found *me*. In fact, my first cat, B.C., was living under the cabin when I moved in, so he came with the house. I liked to think he was the true owner; I was just the tenant. We were happy to welcome him into the house, where he lived for the rest of his thirteen years. A more recent addition to the family, M.C., was living in the woodshed for months before we caught her sneaking into the house through the cat door to eat when we were away. One day, we caught her nonchalantly making her way to the food bowl in broad daylight. She soon moved in and continues to live up to her name of "mystery cat" by surprising us daily with her wild, sweet antics. Like her predecessors, she seems grateful to have found us, but really, we know we're the lucky ones.

While dogs move us out into the world, cats are the epitome of self-containment and discretion, reminding us that it's almost always a good choice to curl up and spend the day sleeping on the couch or stretched out on the deck in the sun. Like Fox, my cats show up daily in my journals, though I've found it challenging to write about any of my animals in a way that doesn't objectify them or slide into sentimentality. In fact, apparently, so many of us have tried to write about our cats that one literary magazine states in its submission guidelines: "Please, no poems about your cat."

Yet, as we know, many famous writers have written poems about cats: Think of Christopher Smart's "For I Will Consider My Cat Jeoffry," or the collection of whimsical poems that T. S. Eliot wrote (interestingly, under a pseudonym): *Old Possum's Book of Practical Cats*. How do we write about our animal companions without lapsing into clichés? Denise Levertov did this through carefully observing her cat, then questioning the very role of metaphor that poets employ, seeing it as another way to objectify the cat. Here's an excerpt from "The Cat as Cat":

> The cat on my bosom
> sleeping and purring
> —fur-petalled, chrysanthemum,
> squirrel-killer—
>
> is a metaphor only if I
> force him to be one,

looking too long in his pale, fond
dilating, contracting eyes

that reject mirrors, refuse
to observe what bides
stockstill.

As I write this, my cat Soot—who also found me—is standing guard next to my laptop, head down, eyes closed, tail neatly wrapped around his front paws. He's a study in gray self-containment. Soot reminds me that he is not a metaphor for anything but who he is: the embodiment of catness.

Our animal companions can remind us simply to be who we are—fully human, with all our imperfections, loved despite our flaws. Those who've been fortunate enough to be "found" by an animal know it creates an indescribable bond. In the simple act of being chosen by an animal that needs us, our connection—to this animal, to ourselves, and to the world—becomes deeper and more enduring.

Contemplation Practices

1. Reflect on how your animal companions found you. Was there an element of serendipity in their arrival in your life?

2. Observe your pet for several minutes without interference. Does this observation slow you down or wind you up? What do you notice that you might not have noticed before? Or what do you notice that particularly endears your pet to you (or, conversely, aggravates you about your pet)?

Writing Practices

1. If you have an animal, write about his or her history in your family. How did the animal come into your life? What does he or she teach you?

2. Start a piece with Thomas's line: "If you were to look into our apartment . . ." (or house or backyard). Describe for the reader what he or she would see at any time of day that includes the animals in your life.

3. As Mark Doty did in "Golden Retrievals," write a piece from an animal's point of view.

4. Try to hone in on a specific, tactile moment with your pet. Describe that moment in detail and see what theme arises to carry you through to other moments, other scenes, a longer story.

5. Write a specific scene from an early memory that has to do with your connection to animals. This can be your own pet, someone else's, or an animal you encountered through school or in a zoo.

Fifteen

Dwelling in Our Bodies

It may be our minds that govern us, our souls that guide us, but it is our bodies on which our histories are written. . . . Instead of regarding ourselves as human beings struggling to have some kind of spiritual experience, perhaps . . . we should consider the possibility that we are spiritual beings having a human experience. And the human experience, as we know, for better or worse, is lived in the body.

—Sharon and Steve Fiffer, *Body*

Brenda

I'm waiting in a white plastic chair for the phlebotomist to draw my blood. He will draw two vials, the rubber tube pinching the flesh of my upper arm. But first he'll run two fingers across the soft skin of my inner elbow, a touch startling in its tenderness, as he nudges my veins to rise to the surface (I'll feel a silly flush of pride when he tells me I have "good veins"). He'll label it and send it off to a lab, where anonymous technicians will dissect this blood down to its smallest parts: my cholesterol level (excellent), my thyroid function (normal), the amounts of vitamin D, B_{12}, and magnesium (low, low, and low). They'll see how much iron I'm carrying, how much sugar. They will print out a map of my blood, a navigational chart that reveals secrets about me even I didn't know.

The body holds lots of secrets. Some of them are ordinary and can be tended to in a physical way (I'll start taking D supplements, for instance, and feel better almost instantly), and others are more ephemeral, more difficult to elucidate. Laraine Herring, in her book *Writing Begins with the Breath,* notes, "Indeed language does come from the mind, but the stories that spring from the authentic voice that is ours and ours alone come from within our own bodies. Our cells have memories. Our bodies have stored all of our experiences—those expressed and unexpressed, even those forgotten. They are there, waiting for us." Our bodies can be wise and wonderful teachers, if we train ourselves to listen.

Sometimes we find ourselves happily in our bodies, completely at home. One of my favorite poems by Linda Gregg, called "Glistening," expresses this quiet joy of the contented body so well:

> As I pull the bucket from the crude well,
> the water changes from dark to a light
> more silver than the sun. When I pour it
> over my body that is standing in the dust
> by the oleander bush, it sparkles easily
> in the sunlight with an earnestness like
> the spirit close up. The water magnifies
> the sun all along the length of it.
> Love is not less because of the spirit.
> Delight does not make the heart childish.
> We thought the blood thinned, our weight
> lessened, that our substance was reduced
> by simple happiness. The oleander is thick
> with leaves and flowers because of spilled

water. Let the spirit marry the heart.
When I return naked to the stone porch,
there is no one to see me glistening.
But I look at the almond tree with its husks
cracking open in the heat. I look down
the whole mountain to the sea. Goats bleating
faintly and sometimes bells. I stand there
a long time with the sun and the quiet,
the earth moving slowly as I dry in the light.

The speaker notices everything: the gradations in the color of the well water, the leaves of the oleander, so vital because of the water spilled like this every day. The entire poem seems a quiet affirmation that yes, we *can* be happy, we *can* be delighted, that such delight in ourselves, our bodies, and our lives "does not make the heart childish." In fact, it makes us fully part of the world. Toward the end of the poem, the speaker—naked, glistening with water and sun, alive from the inside out—is able to take in every detail of her surroundings, such as the "almond tree with its husks / cracking open in the heat," or "goats bleating / faintly and sometimes bells." She is in tune with the wide expanse of time, "the earth moving slowly as I dry in the light."

For me, unfortunately, these transcendent moments don't happen all that frequently. Instead, I think we often move through life literally "beside ourselves"— not fully in the body, ungrounded. As Denise Taylor writes in her essay "Coming Home to the Body,"

The body is tremendously homesick for us, and it waits patiently for our return. Though we have ignored its invitations for years and years, when we do say yes, now, it bounds forward with great exuberance and know-how. We find that we need no training in being fully alive, that we only lacked the determination to feel our aliveness.

I know that for many of us, our bodies have been a source of shame and dissatisfaction, so that's why it can be even more important to acknowledge the body and its effect on our physical and spiritual lives. Stephen Schwartz, in his essay "The Prayer of the Body," writes, "The body only appears to be an enclosure. It is actually a passageway—like an entry to a cave or a cathedral. It is quite the opposite of the way we've been taught to perceive it."

In my first book, *Season of the Body,* I naturally gravitated toward writing about the body, especially because of a key experience that happened when I was a young woman: I had two ectopic pregnancies (embryos that lodge in the fallopian tube), and the resultant miscarriages left me unable to have children. I spent many years in muted grief, not quite sure what I felt: shame, certainly, and a sadness that wouldn't let up, no matter what I tried. I eventually became a massage therapist, trained in a school that believes all our emotions store themselves in the body, and our job is to lure them out into the open. I didn't quite realize that I would be healing my own body and spirit as I turned my intuitive attention toward others.

I ended up writing about that time as a massage therapist, about the way this connection through the body often transcends words. I wrote in the essay "Body Language,"

One time a woman disrobed to reveal a missing breast, the left side of her chest smooth and glossy with scars. We did not speak at all about it, and when she lay down I moved my hand carefully up her calves, then her thighs. I did not ask questions, only whispered the word *breathe* as I headed into the arch of her foot, the declination of her cheekbones.

I touched her chest only at the very end of the massage; I cupped my palms on her sternum, and felt the absence there, an ache traveling up my arm and into my own breast. We both started to cry then: not in a debilitating way, but gently, almost happily, as if we spoke a language of the female, body-to-body, unhampered by the tired obstacle of speech.

This writing led me to explore more directly my own troubled history of my body, though it was difficult to get beyond the weight of grief and shame to write anything that didn't sound like therapy. Then, at last, I found myself writing about one small detail—a needlepoint I stitched while recovering from the miscarriages—as a way into larger emotional and spiritual issues:

As I recovered from surgery, I thought only of that needlepoint, each stitch, one after the other, and mounds of color gradually developed under my hands. . . . [My mother] admired the growing needlepoint, rubbed the bulky fabric between her fingers. . . . She knew that sometimes only the simplest actions are feasible, and those are the ones that lead us out of illness and back into the world. I pulled strands of thread through tiny holes until one day I was able to walk, and one day I was able to laugh, and one day I was able to cry. Recovery, it turned out, was inevitable.

By finding a concrete, neutral object—the needlepoint—on which to focus, I was able to more fully gain perspective and write about that time in a more compassionate and, hopefully, more beautiful way. The essay became about *recovery* more than about the trauma that preceded it. Once we have gained this kind of perspective, we can welcome in all the emotions through the gateway of our bodies, and write about them in ways that help us discover new meaning in our experiences.

Holly

Maybe because I'm Pisces, or maybe because my parents set me loose in a lake—strapped into water wings—as soon as I could walk, I've always felt at home in water. I'm never more in my body than when I'm swimming, slipping through the water like a seal. This is when I feel most alive, especially when there's nothing between me and the cool, silky glide of water. Growing up in Minnesota, I found plenty of lakes to swim in and spent many sticky August days immersed in their cool waters, many warm nights skinny-dipping under the round eye of the moon.

Since both my parents loved to swim, most of our family vacations were spent at a lake. My father's swimming ritual consisted of his evening "smoke dip" after dinner. My three sisters and I would watch, giggling, as he waded into the water with his pipe clenched in his teeth, then carefully breaststroked up the shore, trailing pipe smoke behind him. Summers, when I was home from college, he'd knock on my bedroom door at 6 a.m. We'd slip quietly down the stairs, out the door, and across the street to the lake. When we'd return, he'd go to work and I'd sometimes go back to bed, but I'd had my swim and the day was complete.

All my mother's life—but especially toward the end of it, when she had Alzheimer's disease—she was never happier than when she was swimming. I remember one visit in particular when my parents were vacationing on Sanibel Island. After losing a battle with my mother at the grocery store—where she kept putting bars of chocolate in the pockets of her cardigan sweater—we came back to the hotel and I suggested, out of desperation, going for a swim. I remember watching her breaststroke back and forth, back and forth, in the small lima-bean-shaped hotel pool, her face lit up with pleasure.

When I went to Alaska, I had to trade in my love of swimming in clear, cool lakes for the colder, salty tang of the sea. A summer in Alaska is never complete without diving in at least once. It's a ritual that connects me with my body, reminds me that thousands of years ago, our ancestors came out of the sea, crawled ashore. Perhaps that's why swimming feels so nourishing, so restorative—one is immersed again in life-giving waters. Suspended in clear water, it's easy to imagine a life without limits.

Though swimming makes me dream of living without boundaries, we dwell in the vessel of our body. When I'm spending too many hours at my desk grading student papers, I try to remember to look up, where a quote thumb-tacked above my desk reminds me: "If you don't take care of your body, where will you live?" Don't we all forget this, caught up in our busy lives, racing from one meeting, one appointment to the next? I allow myself, then, to stand up, stretch, walk around my studio or even around the block. When I sit down again, I'm more fully back in my body—and my mind, too, is more alert, ready to resume its work.

Being with the breath invites us to do this. As we draw in each breath, we follow it into our body, focusing on all the sensations of breathing in. This simple act reminds us to come back to our body, to lean over and listen closely, carefully, as we would to our best friend. As we breathe in, we note the sensation of the cool, life-giving air entering our nostrils, moving down and filling our lungs. We can then follow the breath going out, leaving our body, letting go with each exhalation, releasing each breath with a small sigh. As we follow each breath in and out, we become aware of any tension in our body. Now we might notice that familiar knot between our shoulder blades, the tightness in our neck, the stiffness in our knees and hips from sitting too long. This practice encourages us to return to our bodies in each moment, to breathe into the knots, to acknowledge the stiffness like an old friend, to welcome even these as a bittersweet reminder that, yes, we dwell in our bodies.

I'm lucky to live close to a lake, so each summer I swim as often as possible. But the swims at the end of summer are the most memorable. Immersed in tea-colored water, I watch iridescent bubbles trail off my fingers and vanish into the murky depths below. I swim overhand to warm up, turning my head rhythmically to breathe. With each breath I catch a glimpse of blue sky, a green fringe of leafy aspens, then I dip my face back down in the translucent amber water. For me, then—and, I suspect, for many of us who love this exercise—swimming becomes a form of meditation. I'm breathing *in and out, in and out*, focusing on my breath until I'm not aware of anything but the sensation of my arms moving through the water, of my legs kicking rhythmically, of the cold water chilling my belly. I once tried to capture this in a poem called "Swimming into Fall." Here's an excerpt:

> and in this way
> I swim back into summer
> holding on with each stroke,
> each exhaling drift of bubbles
> until the water is swimming me
> in its golden fins and at last
> I can breathe without sadness,
> fall, and one season tilting into the next
> as they do and this could be enough:
> to move without thought
> where sun mottles shadow.

Swimming slows time for those minutes you're submerged in the water, when everything else falls away, and you can feel the earth slowly turning, the tides flooding and ebbing. Whenever I can't see my way clear, I head for the closest bay, lake, or pool and swim until the knots loosen, and I'm once more gliding through the world, a fish, or maybe even a swan, at home again in my body.

Contemplation Practices

1. For a few minutes in meditation, practice focusing on the gap between your breaths. Try not to hold your breath, but merely observe the natural rhythms of the breath: in, pause, out, pause, in. . . . Do this for about five minutes, and then return to easy focus on the breath itself.

2. Do a "body scan" while lying on the floor, acknowledging each part of your body, allowing it to relax and feel supported by the ground. Breathe deeply, especially into those parts of the body that seem to hold on and resist.

3. Think of a physical activity that brings you back into your body. Perhaps it is swimming, as it is for Holly. Or it might be running in the park, walking on a sandy beach, going to the gym, or playing pickup basketball. Whatever it is, the next time you do this activity, consider it an active meditation for a few minutes at a time—being fully in your body, aware of all the sensations.

Writing Practices

1. Consider a moment in your life when you felt fully in your body. This may have taken place during childhood or more recently. As Linda Gregg did in her poem "Glistening," create the scene on the page, focusing on the physical details of both your body and your surroundings.

2. Write a short prose piece or a poem that focuses specifically on the body in action, perhaps in the activity you identified above.

3. Think of an occasion when your body failed you. As Brenda did in her essay

"Needlepoint," try to remember a small object from that time which will help you explore a difficult period in the life of your body.

4. The essayist David James Duncan provides us with a wonderful example of how physical activity, like sports, can be contemplation in motion. In this bit from his essay "The Mickey Mantle Koan," Duncan is playing catch with his older brother, an activity they did frequently, but one that takes on new importance in retrospect, after his brother had died:

> Genuine catch-playing occurs in a double-limbo between busyness and idleness, and between the imaginary and the real. As with any contemplative pursuit, it takes time, and the ability to forget time, to slip into this dual limbo, and to discover (i.e. lose) oneself in the music of the game. . . . As our movements became fluid and the throws brisk and accurate, the pretense of practice would inevitably fade, and we'd just aim for the chest and fire, *hisssss pop! hisssss pop!* till a meal, a duty or total darkness forced us to recall that this is the world in which even timeless pursuits come to an end.

This reflection, full of sensory details (the hiss/pop of the ball), allows us to see how physical activity can lead us into the world of the spirit.

Are there sports you enjoy watching or playing—or that you played when you were younger? How could you write about this sport through a contemplative lens? How did you pay attention in such an intensely active way? Try writing a scene in which an ordinary activity—like playing catch or throwing a Frisbee—leads you to greater insight about something that troubles you. Zero in on one specific, small object from that time.

Sixteen

Responding to Art

There are moments in our lives, there are moments in a day, when we seem to see beyond the usual—become clairvoyant. . . . Such are the moments of our greatest happiness. Such are the moments of our greatest wisdom.

—Robert Henri, *The Art Spirit*

Brenda

I'm in an Ikebana class, learning the Japanese art of flower arranging, and I'm sitting in front of a single tulip, trying to decide the exact angle to place its stem in the shallow vase. After our instructor demonstrates, we choose our branches, eye the flowers, try to discern the strong curves or lines that draw our eye, then snip away anything that gets in the way. For me (and for all the students), the challenge is always not to do too much, to resist the impulse to fill in all that blank space with color or line. We need to trust emptiness, to allow space to do its work.

The Book of Flowers (the "bible" of Ikebana) describes it this way: "Ikebana is an act of space—the space between branches, the space between flowers and leaves, and the space between masses. In other words, the space between flowers and branches comes alive." Ikebana is a contemplative art practiced intuitively, and the creations reveal a person's state of mind. As the author, Kadensho, puts it: "Ikebana settings must maintain a balance between the perfection of technique and the imperfection of the human heart." This is good advice for writing, too, and when I'm practicing Ikebana, I feel myself training my writing mind as well. I'm slowing down, trying to discern which details are essential and which are not.

"Ikebana is a world of encounters," the *Book of Flowers* says. "This is what Ikebana means—always facing the flowers with candor and listening to what they say. The heart must open wide to do this." When I do Ikebana, I feel my artistic mind opening along with my heart, ready to do my writing with the same attitude of respectful listening.

When I'm in the presence of any art—music, Ikebana, painting, or dance—I find new inspiration for my own work. It becomes a collaboration, though the artist may be long gone. For instance, the very first essay I ever wrote, "Prologue to a Sad Spring," was a response to an Edward Weston photograph that had hooked itself into my imagination. I began with simple description, then moved on to ask why:

I've put a new picture on my wall, a photograph bought for me at an Edward Weston exhibit last April. The composition shows a young woman, all in black, posed against a high, white fence. She half turns toward the camera; her right hand lies tentatively across her heart. The shadow of a leafless tree (I imagine it to be a young oak) curves up and over this slight figure. Actually, it does more than curve; the tree arches across the tall fence in a gesture of protection. Almost a bow of respect.

A wide-brimmed hat, trimmed in flowers, overshadows the woman's face, but I can make out the line of her small chin, the pensive set of her mouth. She seems to gaze at some person beyond the camera, someone who moves away quite rapidly, and she can't quite decide whether to follow. It is a moment of suppressed panic. Even in her frame, the woman appears to tremble.

Why do I like this picture so much? I glance at it every day, and every day it puzzles me. What draws me to those dark, shaded eyes? What holds me transfixed by the movement of gray shadows over the straight white planks, the drape of the black coat, the white hand raised to the breast in a stunned gesture of surprise or healing?

Art allows us the opportunity to practice observing and describing small details. Our description often becomes a mirror—I naturally project my own thoughts and emotions on this figure in the photograph. The question "Why?" leads me through a history of lost love in a short essay that scrutinizes the photo for clues. In the end, I notice not the woman but the way the tree's shadow has deepened under my gaze. After mulling on the power of the black-and-white image, I zero in on this small detail to end the piece:

Perhaps this woman is really dressed all in red, and the fence behind her painted a bright blue. The shadows would not be so alluring, then; I don't think I would care quite so much. As it is, I find the tree's shadow to be the most intriguing part of the picture. It has the most mystery to it, and the most promise. With the strong curve of the trunk, the sinuous movement of the limbs overhead, the tree forms a vigilant presence, a sentinel. The oak dominates the scene, carries all the light, draws the eye to this woman, who, in her preoccupation, keeps looking the opposite way.

Art allows us to look long and hard, to stop time in order to examine with compassion our preoccupations, our obsessions, our desires. We can enter art in a way that we cannot enter life, since life is constantly changing, moving fast, slipping from our grasp. If we develop the patience to sit with it, art will open the space for us to respond with great work of our own.

Holly

I'm sitting on a hard wooden pew in the chapel at Bastyr University, resting in the lofty spaces and otherworldly music of the ProMusica "Navidad" concert. Our friend Laura sings in the choir, so this has become one of our cherished holiday traditions, so much so that John and I embarked on a rough trip by ferry, then struggled up an icy hill, despite a weather forecast calling for more cold temperatures and snow. Several times we wanted to turn back, but each time the memory of how much we enjoyed previous concerts kept us pressing on.

Now that we're here, relaxing in the arms of this exquisite music, I'm thankful we continued our journey. Since we're at the afternoon performance, light streams through the floor-to-ceiling stained-glass widows, shattering in an intricate, abstract pattern on the floor. Ahead of me, above the altar, is an enormous gold starburst, gold rays shooting out in every direction. Zillions of tiny gold tiles line the altar on either side, flanked by two columns adorned with birds and flowers.

But it's the *space* I'm loving, the vaulted ceiling above me, at this moment filled with the ethereal voices of the Women's Schola choir singing "Ave Maria" a cappella. *Ah, yes.* This *is why we traveled all this way.* At last, my busy mind can rest in this stillness.

How difficult it is to make time and space in our days for beauty and music, and yet how necessary. Most of the ancient civilizations created festivals of light to remind people that light, beauty, and music are as integral to our lives as breathing and eating. And if we can't make space for this, even if it means simply listening to beautiful music, how much harder to make space in our hearts for what's sacred.

We need music, art, and poetry to remind us that it's essential to carve out space for silence and beauty. In her book *Distracted: The Erosion of Attention and the Coming Dark Age*, Maggie Jackson points out that we can now "tap into 50 million websites, 1.8 million books in print, 75 million blogs. . . . We can contact millions of people across the globe, yet we increasingly connect with even our most intimate friends and family via instant messaging, virtual visits, and fleeting meetings that are rescheduled a half dozen times." The problem with this, she goes on to say, is that "the way we live is eroding our capacity for deep, sustained, perceptive attention—the building block of intimacy, wisdom, and cultural progress."

Because our lives have become driven by technology, perhaps art and music, which nurture a deeper level of attention, are more essential than ever. Even though we can listen to music on our iPods whenever we want, have entire art galleries on our desktops, does that equal the experience of sustained, focused listening or looking? Without giving into the busyness, perhaps we can find ways to rest, briefly, whenever we can.

I'm reminded of the last stanza of a poem by Rilke that begins with the lines: "My life is not this steeply sloping hour / in which you see me hurrying." He articulates the paradox of being able to rest in what he calls the "dark intervals":

> I am the rest between two notes,
> which are somehow always in discord. . . .
> And the song goes on, beautiful.

Returning to the music in this chapel, I hear a litany repeated again and again, insistent, demanding my attention. I turn to the program notes, read that this piece was written by Alberto Grau, a Venezuelan composer known for placing ecological concerns at the heart of his music. The phrase is *Kasar mie la gaji*, which means "The earth is tired" in Hausa, the language of the inhabitants of the African Sahel. I'm reminded then that we need space, too, for what's difficult to take in, for messages like this. Karen, the conductor, explains that it's common in the Sahel region for people to inquire of each other by asking if they are tired. *No, I'm not tired* is the acceptable response. So to say this on behalf of the earth is even more poignant. At the end, we all sit motionless in the silence, taking it in.

And now I watch as, one last time, Karen holds this intangible space in both her arms, almost still, then lifts them slowly as the last piece ends, the sweet, sad notes hanging in the air so tangibly we can almost see their fluid, golden sheen. Even at the darkest, busiest time of the year, I'm reminded to create space for what is beautiful, for what is sacred, and for what is difficult, too. We can turn to music and art to sustain our spirit, to hold the light, to give us space and inspiration when we need it most.

Contemplation Practices

1. Is there an art form other than writing that draws you into the contemplative frame of mind? Try to practice a particular art—music, painting, flower arrangement, cooking—in a contemplative manner.

2. Each week, block off time to create space for something that inspires you, whether it's listening to music, looking at art, creating a beautiful centerpiece, or designing a container garden. Make a commitment to this time/space by writing it on your calendar, honoring it the way you would any

other appointment. In her book *The Artist's Way,* Julia Cameron emphasizes that we need to make "artist's dates" in order to nurture the artistic frame of mind.

Writing Practices

1. Write a poem or a short essay in response to a painting or photograph you love or a piece of music you find inspiring. Or write a piece in response to your garden, or a beautiful meal. Use this as an opportunity to keep observing beyond the surface details, to notice something unexpected.

2. Put on your favorite music and listen to it without doing anything else except freewriting the images that the music evokes. Then write a poem or short essay from these images.

3. Imitate Rilke's poem ("I am the rest between two notes . . .") by beginning a poem or essay with the line: "I am the _____." Fill in the blank with details from some art you love: a piece of music, a painting, a dance, and so on. Continue the piece by repeating, "I am the _____," picking up more details as you go.

Seventeen

Allowing Emptiness

> Whatever art offered the men and women of previous eras, what it offers our own, is space—a certain breathing room for the spirit.
>
> —John Updike

Brenda

I recently hired a team of professional organizers to help me deal with what I've come to call my "room of shame": the second bedroom in my house, literally overflowing with ancient files, books, out-of-season clothes, a thousand paper clips, broken speakers, chargers to things that don't even exist anymore, sleeping bags, dog crates—everything that couldn't find a place elsewhere. When I realized I hadn't even set foot in that room in a month—that the heaviness of that room was making me grumpy—I knew I had to do something.

So two cheerful women in blue aprons bustled into my house, and within two hours they had transformed that room—and, as a consequence, the space in my mind. They did so in ways I could never have envisioned. They efficiently boxed up papers and books, hauled out oversized furniture into the carport, and coached me as I cleaned out a horrifying desk drawer. They grouped "like with like," and by the time they were done, I felt as though the room was really breathing for the first time in ten years.

Their motto is "Experience Clarity," and it's true; I felt like *I* could breathe easier—freed from the weight of all those unruly things. Now I sit and work in this transformed room all the time, accompanied by a feeling of deep contentment.

This feeling of spaciousness is something I've often intuitively created in my writing as well. I've learned—even without the ladies in the blue aprons looking over me—that I have to allow more emptiness in the work itself; I need to de-clutter. This often takes the form of white space in my essays: fragments, small pieces surrounded by emptiness. I've come to befriend what is unspoken as well as what is voiced. Sometimes silence really does speak louder than words. Once I have raw material to work with, I keep pruning and pruning. In this way, I hope my work takes on a more meditative, contemplative quality—for both me and my reader. I hope that it breathes.

For example, in one of the first essays I ever wrote, "A Thousand Buddhas," I wrote about my work as a massage therapist, but I didn't know why. I knew there was some grief, some unanswerable question, at the heart of all this. I pieced together small sections that made no sense on their own, but once in a constellation with the others began to accumulate into new meaning. The white space, the silence, allowed for that uncertainty.

I needed to trust my intuition, to take my time, to allow other images, such as the birth of my godson, to become part of the piece. I needed time to understand that my own miscarriages were a part of this story as well. In the end, this essay—only ten pages long, with much blankness taking up that space—took me over a year to write. I needed to practice patience, *being* instead of doing. As John D'Agata, an editor for the *Seneca Review*, puts it, these kinds of essays—often called "lyric essays" because of the way they resemble poetry—have a "built-in mechanism for provoking meditation. They require us to complete their meaning."

The process of putting together a lyric essay, or a book composed of small sections and white space, text and silence, can be a contemplative practice that slows down the relentless forward push of traditional narrative and instead allows some breathing room, some simplification.

For instance, in her memoir of grief, *Safekeeping*, Abigail Thomas writes a series of short vignettes that together explore the complicated emotions she feels at the death of her second husband, a man to whom she is no longer married. She addresses him directly in the second chapter, titled "Offering," which is only a single paragraph, set in the middle of the page:

> While you were alive the past was a live unfinished thing. Like a painting we weren't done with. Like a garden we were still learning to tend. Nothing was set in stone yet, and weren't we ourselves still changing? We might redeem our past by redeeming ourselves. I had in mind a sort of alchemy. But then you died, and just like that, it was over. What was done was done. Now we could never fix it. All I can do is chip away, see what comes off in my hand, look for a shape.

Emptiness surrounds her words and creates a small island. Coupled with the title, "Offering," the words seem literally "offered" to the reader in the narrator's cupped hands. It's a small gift, and as we unwrap it, we are allowed an intimate glimpse into the speaker's thoughts and emotions. She writes short, fragmented sentences; there is nothing superfluous, nothing inessential. She has only a short time to get her thoughts across, and so each line, each word, counts. She creates a sense of space even between lines: "Like a painting we weren't done with. Like a garden we were still learning to tend." We move from one image to the next, but with a pause in between, mimicking the mind's (and the breath's) rhythms. She ends in a metaphor that articulates what she will be up to here: "All I can do is chip away, see what comes off in my hand, look for a shape."

The book that unfolds from this initial offering enacts this "chipping away," and we, the readers, peer over her shoulder as the bits and pieces assemble themselves into a story of complicated love and grief, a story that simply could not be told any other way. It's all she can do.

Peggy Shumaker, in *Just Breathe Normally* (her memoir of recovery from brain injury), gives her readers a similar "offering" to start her fragmented story. The book itself mimics the process by which her memory returned—in slivers—and the starting point for this narrative offers us a single scene that seems unrelated, but that provides a metaphor for her entire experience. It is titled "Just This Once," and is just two paragraphs long. It begins,

Once, in a wild place, I felt myself quiet down. I listened, drew silent breaths. It was dangerous not to warn the bears I was there, no question. But I wanted to live one moment in a wild place without disturbing the other creatures there. This delicate moment laced with fear—a life wish.

Just this once, I told myself. Everyone else snored. Black nets billowed, let in a few mosquitoes.

The entire scene is infused with space, with silence, with the tension created between beauty and fear. The lines are short, succinct, with a quality of being whispered in our ear so as not to disturb the moment. "Just this once, I told myself." She leaves the cabin and quietly walks toward the edge of the water, where tracks show the presence of bear. She ends the chapter in a crystalline image: "Undisturbed and not disturbing, I stood still breathing in sphagnum's mossy sigh quiet after loon calls, followed unmarked paths left by stars too wild to show themselves anywhere but here, inhaled the nursing musk, the bear I knew was there."

We leave the narrator there, in the presence of danger, in this "delicate moment laced with fear," the thrilling beauty created from the encounter of opposites. The entire scene is filled with images of breathing, of settling into the breath and the space between breaths. We don't know the outcome, but we suspect the narrator emerges unharmed. And transformed. With this image, we then embark on Shumaker's journey of injury and recovery, a process in which she will also encounter her deepest fears and be changed by them. Sometimes this kind of story can only be told with a great deal of space to hold us. One deep breath after another.

Holly

For my "small noticing" this morning, I'm watching lovely, soft flakes of snow drift outside the window of my writing studio, covering the shiny green leaves of salal, Oregon grape, coating even the thin leaves of the bamboo. The fence posts wear caps of white and a few winter wrens hop around, searching for stray seeds. I love the way snow simplifies our choices: I was scheduled to go to Seattle for a dentist appointment—cancelled—a meeting at the college—cancelled—a visit with friends—rescheduled. Suddenly the day is as open and choiceless as the snow coating the grass, and I'm elated to be home with nothing scheduled but reading, writing, walking—even enough time to make soup and bake bread.

Watching the snow fall, I'm reminded of the winter I spent near Ely, Minnesota, working at an environmental learning center with sixth graders from Minneapolis–St. Paul schools. After spending the week teaching them to snowshoe and cross-country ski, we took them on an overnight winter camping expedition, sleeping in a snow cave we'd built out of blocks of ice. I remember making our way home across the windswept lake, stopping to listen as the local timber wolves howled to each other from ridge to ridge, their wild chorus echoing across the frozen lake.

That winter, I was struck by how snow simplifies the landscape and therefore, too, the mind. That stark, monochromatic landscape allowed my mind to rest, allowed me to see the subtle shades of color I might otherwise have missed—the rose tips of birch and alder beginning to bud as spring arrived, all the gradations of green in moss and lichen, delicate as lace. Snow reminds us to simplify our lives, literally and metaphorically, by reducing the world to just what matters.

When we can do this, both in our writing and our lives, we find that there's more room, that the emptiness isn't so empty, that a vacant lot is not so vacant. Patricia Nerison's poem "Before the Solstice" does this.

> In the soft gloom of a still, gray morning
> trees gather themselves
> listening to winter emptiness.
>
> I listen, too—and hear
> whispers in the vacant lot next door
> as if cello bows were stroking stalks of fescue,
>
> —and see no vacancy
> but a dozen robins tuning their wings
> in puddles of yesterday's rain.

This poem depicts a simple winter landscape and shares with us the poet's revelation: Instead of vacancy, she hears "whispers . . . / as if cello bows were stroking stalks of fescue," sees "a dozen robins tuning their wings / in puddles of yesterday's rain." Notice how even the "trees gather themselves / listening to winter emptiness." The poet includes just that one image before sharing her revelation with the reader. As writers, we can train ourselves to see this way, to look beyond the expected to see what's really present. Robert Michael Pyle, author of many award-winning natural history books, asks a question in *Walking the High Ridge* that's stayed with me: "What's less vacant than a vacant lot to the curious mind?"

How much space do we need to feel spacious? As the poet Gensei puts it in "Poem Without a Category,"

> The point in life is to know what's enough. . . .
> With the happiness held in one inch-square heart
> you can fill the whole space between heaven and earth.

Just as the snow falling outside my window simplifies my choices today, I'm reminded that I, too, can create more space in my life, whether by cancelling appointments or even literally de-cluttering my space. I read a piece in the *Seattle Times/PI Northwest* magazine about Dee Williams, a woman in Seattle, who lives in an eighty-four-square-foot house built on a flatbed trailer parked in a friend's backyard. She gave away all but a few belongings—just what she needed to live.

I now live in a small cabin—seven hundred square feet (a mansion compared to eighty-four square feet) and for four years lived on a thirty-six-foot sailboat, so I know how to simplify my belongings. Yet, I know we all have some possessions we are reluctant to give up. For me, it's my books, which have overflowed the shelves and rest in piles on the floor. I resolve to spend an hour culling them, and then go through my closet, remembering the clothes swap a friend organized for later this month. I'll bring the pair of pants that, hard as it is to admit, no longer fits, the dress I bought on sale but have no occasion to wear, the out-of-style cardigan sweater, a gift from my mother many years ago. At the swap, we'll bring a dish to share, eat and laugh together, then dump our contributions in the middle of the room. Several hours later, I'll leave with a wool vest that is new to me, and my clothes, too, will have found new homes.

Meanwhile it's lunchtime, and black bean soup simmers on the stove while a round loaf of Swedish rye bread rises in the kitchen. Later, I'll take Fox on a walk down to the beach, and I'll find other friends and neighbors out walking, too, friends I haven't seen in months. We'll decide to meet for dinner, share our respective pots of soup, catch up on each other's lives. As the day unfolds in the same slow, lovely way the snowflakes drift down, I can't help but dream of a snow day once a month—a day when we can unplug from the frenetic demands of our lives, when we can enjoy our neighbors and our community, rediscover—and appreciate—whatever's within walking distance. We can learn to make more room, to value what's held in the empty spaces in our days and trust that vacancy will yield insight.

Contemplation Practices

1. Consider your living space and how you might make it even more spacious. Are there possessions you might give away or recycle that would enable you to appreciate your space more and encourage a clearer mind? What could you do without?

2. Consider organizing a clothes swap/potluck in your community as a way to de-clutter and connect with friends, too. Or consider hiring an organizer; it's amazing what a professional can do in a short time, and you'll feel so much lighter afterward.

3. Declare a snow day—stay home and make soup, make space to think about what you value in your community, and how you might spend more time with your neighbors.

Writing Practices

1. Reflect on these lines from Rainier Maria Rilke: "Whoever you are: some evening take a step out of your house, which you know so well. Enormous space is near." Try taking a step outside of your house or apartment some evening and write about the "enormous space" you find.

2. Take a piece of writing you've started and see how you might simplify it—remove extraneous details until you can see the bare bones of the piece. Then put on just enough flesh to give it form. (If you're using Microsoft Word, sometimes it's interesting to use the "Auto-summarize" function to see what the program picks out as "most important." It gives you a highly objective—and sometimes quite funny—view of the bare bones of your piece!)

3. As Patricia Nerison did, visit a vacant lot in your neighborhood and write about what you find. Look and listen hard. Try to see what's really there, then capture it in just a few well-chosen images.

4. Write an essay or poem in short fragments and spend time rearranging these fragments to see the effect of ordering. Or take a piece you've already written and cut it apart, put the pieces on the floor, and walk among them. See what you can do as you rearrange them and put space between the scenes. Use *Just Breathe Normally* or *Safekeeping* as a model.

Eighteen

On Mortality

Ah, Beloved, do you see those orange lilies?
They knew my mother,
But who belonging to me will they know
When I am gone.
—Amy Lowell, "The Garden by Moonlight"

Brenda

It seems that the older I get, the more I understand the way mortality shapes our perception and our willingness to be fully in this world. It's not something I used to think about directly—too scary—but now I often find myself reading the obituaries, musing on what I would want my own to say: What are the things that will sum up my life? What will stand out? I know this sounds a little morbid, but as Mother Theresa has said: "Each of us is merely a small instrument; all of us, after accomplishing our mission, will disappear." I wonder what small things people will remember: my dinner parties on the deck? My love for my dog? My weird obsession with cooking magazines? Will they remember my writing, my teaching, or will they remember a particular morning with coffee, a conversation that delved deeper than expected?

We can't really know. All we can do is keep learning, until the very end, how to live an authentic life. How to be really *here*. And we can look to others as teachers in this lesson.

My next-door neighbor, Winton Manley, is just such a teacher for me: He's ninety-eight years old and still drives his own car. I see him in the afternoons, backing out of the driveway, swerving a little wildly sometimes, but he always makes it safely into the street, then putters away in his white Oldsmobile to wherever it is he needs to go. He takes care of things. He takes care of his wife, Dorothy, who is ninety-four and has such bad arthritis now that she can't move without her walker. "I have to persuade her to get up," Winton says to me sometimes, when he walks over to admire my petunias or my pansies. "There are good days and there are bad days."

I remember so clearly a day last summer, when I saw the two of them sitting out on their new deck in the sun. (Winton had it built because Dorothy can't get out into her garden anymore; here she can admire her pots of geraniums.) The light glinted off their white, white hair. They were just sitting and smiling, not saying a word, and when I finally waved to announce my presence, Dorothy gazed at me as if I were just the most blessed creature on the planet. Her face looked translucent with love, with her expectation that I was exactly what the doctor ordered.

"A beautiful day!" she exclaimed, in a voice that's grown so wavery in the years I've lived next door. I echoed her, speaking as loudly as I could: "Yes, a beautiful day!" And because I was on my way to my own back patio to do who knows what—some reading, some weeding—and because it would have been exhausting to keep talking in that loud, hearty voice, I just waved again and continued on, leaving them sitting there, nodding, enjoying their beautiful day.

And I know that sometime soon, their daughter or grandson will come to my door and tell me that one or both of them has "passed." And I know I'll gasp and say, "I'm sorry," because I *am*: sorry not only for their passing, and for a daughter's grief, a grandson's pain, but truly sorry for all my moments of inattention, my reluctance to keep talking a few minutes longer, my unwillingness to walk the few steps necessary to chat. I'll remember all the cucumbers and green beans Winton left on my doorstep—bags of them, more than a single woman could ever eat—and I'll wish, so heartily, that I'd had even a sliver of such abundance to return.

There's a poem I love by Miguel de Unamuno called "Throw Yourself Like Seed." In it he exclaims,

> Shake off this sadness, and recover your spirit;
> sluggish you will never see the wheel of fate
> that brushes your heel as it turns going by,
> the man who wants to live is the man in whom life is abundant. . . .
>
> Throw yourself like seed as you walk, and into your own field,
> don't turn your face for that would be to turn it to death,
> and do not let the past weigh down your motion.

When I consider my life as one defining moment after another, I see that I am most fully alive when I "throw myself like seed," not holding back. I ask myself: What am I holding in reserve? Why? So I take this as my lesson, allowing Winton and Dorothy to be my unexpected teachers: As much as we can, we must never pass up the opportunity to connect, to be fully with each other and with the world, to make each day beautiful for the time we have.

Holly

Until I turned forty-six, it was easy to imagine that growing old was something that happened to others, that death was a long way off. While I hope death *is* a long way off, I'm coming to accept that it will happen to me, that none of us—no matter how healthy or fit—will escape it and that, much as we might wish, we won't be able to choose our departure.

When I turned forty-six, I lost my mother to Alzheimer's disease. She'd always been in good physical shape, practiced yoga before anyone else I knew, and even when she was in her sixties still loved to bike, swim, and hike. She kept her mind active, too, going back to college to learn French and study philosophy after her four daughters moved away from home. As is often the case with this terrible disease, her death was a slow process of subtraction; we lost her cell by cell, synapse by synapse, over ten years. Because we lost her slowly, her death was a kind of relief for us, and, I hope, for her. When she died, she returned to us as our mother—even if only in memory—no longer the stranger she'd become.

Knowing her experience, I began to consider both death and life differently. Her last gift was the reminder to live in the present. Because she could no longer remember her past or imagine a future, she lived fully in the moment, delighting in the red cardinals at the feeder, in the squirrel sneaking up to steal birdseed. The clear evidence, not just of mortality but of the possibility I will be afflicted by a similar disease, made me think more deeply about my own actions. While I'd tried to remind myself to live in the present, I tended to do so only when it was easy, like at a meditation retreat. Now, my mother's voice followed me everywhere, reminding me not just to live in the present but to appreciate every robin I see, to exclaim over every sunset as she would.

Ten years later, I'm still grateful to my mother for this last reminder—and to others who continue to remind me. This week, my former journalism teacher and friend Rags is visiting. Rags has lived and traveled all over the world—he shipped out on a freighter for South America at seventeen—so perhaps it's not so surprising that he's still game for adventure at ninety-seven. (Several years ago, he traveled alone to Mozambique to visit his daughter and son-in-law.) He had a stroke two years ago that affected his balance, so his gait, which used to be lithe and quick is now slow and shuffling, though he still moves with great dignity. On this visit, I promised him we'll have dinner with friends, visit Port Gamble, go to the Rose Theater, and eat at the Silverwater Cafe in Port Townsend. "Oh, a vacation!" he said.

As we spend these days together, I marvel at the patience and acceptance he needs now: patience for how long it takes to move across a room, acceptance that he can no longer read. But his memory is as sharp as ever, and as we sit together in the flickering light of the fire, he remembers the blackouts in London, where he was stationed as a foreign correspondent during World War II, recalls how the war was an elixir, how it made him—and everyone—grateful to be alive. Those who know him intimately know he's never lost that spirit, know how it's served him well over all the years of his very full life.

Even now, he insists on living in his own home, alone, despite offers from his three daughters to come live with them. When I try to help with the small tasks that consume much of his day, he gently refuses: "If I am to keep living at home, I must be able to do these things myself." We all know that his independent spirit is what keeps him here with us, alive and still vital at ninety-seven.

Years ago, when Rags and I were driving to his cabin on Harstene Island, we hit a deer. It was a dark night, rain pelting down, when we came around the curve to face the deer standing on the road. There were no other cars on the road, so Rags swerved and almost missed him—just struck a glancing blow—and the deer leapt off into the woods. We pulled over, parked, and stumbled into the dark, wet woods, trying to find its trail, wanting to know the deer wasn't suffering. After tramping through the woods for an hour without finding it, we hoped that meant the deer had survived uninjured. We drove more slowly then, chastened.

As much as we try to avoid these brushes with death—and for good reason —in other cultures, death is not sequestered so neatly from life. As part of training his monks, the Buddha used to take them to the graveyard so they could practice being with death—and these graveyards were less antiseptic than ours; there, the monks would find bones, tangible reminders that this life is fleeting. How would we live if that knowledge informed every moment?

Rags has always loved the coming of evening, or what he loves to call *l'heure bleu*, so last night, I read him Jane Kenyon's beautiful poem "Let Evening Come." Her poem, both a chant and an invocation, springs from an awareness of her own body's mortality—she was facing death from cancer at a relatively young age when she wrote it—so the surrender implicit in her images takes on a deep, poignant resonance.

> Let the light of late afternoon
> shine through the chinks in the barn, moving
> up the bales as the sun moves down.
>
> Let the cricket take up the chafing
> as a woman takes up her needles
> and her yarn. Let evening come.
>
> Let dew collect on the hoe abandoned
> in long grass. Let the stars appear
> and the moon disclose her silver horn.

Let the fox go back to its sandy den.
Let the wind die down. Let the shed
go black inside. Let evening come.

To the bottle in the ditch, to the scoop
in the oats, to the air in the lung
let evening come.

Let it come, as it will, and don't
be afraid. God does not leave us
comfortless, so let evening come.

Kenyon's images create a gentle exhortation to the reader (and to the poet; it feels like she's murmuring to herself) to let go, to allow the world to be the world, going about its business, as we move inexorably toward our own vanishing. She focuses on the small details, the poet as witness to the small shafts of light that make their way through the darkness of the barn, moving "up the bales as the sun moves down," the two contrary motions showing the exquisite, see-sawing balance at the heart of our lives. We hear the crickets, we see dew as it gathers, and we hear the wind go quiet, until finally all this observation leads us back to the body, to the "air in the lung." The poet tells us "don't be afraid," that we are never alone or "comfortless" if we allow ourselves to be fully present to the divinity in each moment of life. We must let "it" come: evening, the night, our own body's mortality.

When I look up, Rags is dozing, halfway in the spirit world, and I'm filled with gratitude for his wise presence. By delighting in each small detail of the world going about its business—this lesson I've learned many times over the years from Rags—I hope to find acceptance of my body slowing down, my own inevitable mortality. May we have the courage and wisdom that Rags embodies —and that poets like Jane Kenyon remind us of—to "let evening come."

Contemplation Practices

1. Dedicate a contemplative practice session or two to an elder who has had an influence in your life. Keep a picture on your altar and allow his or her presence to infuse your practice space.

2. Interview an elder you are close to: What is he or she grateful for? What are you grateful for in your relationship with this person? Tell this person what he or she has taught you.

3. If you are an elder, consider what gifts you have to offer to your community. What insights can you share with your family and friends? Seek out ways that you can pass along your well-earned wisdom, ways to connect with those younger who don't have your rich life experience. Don't wait for an invitation—invite your grandchildren or your neighbors for tea some rainy afternoon and share your stories.

4. As Brenda did, reflect on your legacy—what do you wish to be remembered for when you're gone? Make it a conscious practice to reflect on this question periodically as a way of helping to define your own life's purpose, of staying on course with what matters most.

Writing Practices

1. Invite an elder to share his or her stories, then write them down—in his or her words—in the form of a poem or story in that person's voice.

2. Write a specific scene that shows your observation of an elder doing some-

thing he or she loves (this can be as simple as sitting on the back deck, puttering in the kitchen, or reading a book). Paying attention fully—and rendering this attention in writing—is a way of paying homage.

3. Write an imitation of Jane Kenyon's poem "Let Evening Come" simply by repeating the word *Let* at the beginning of every line. What do you imagine you would like to "let" happen as you near the end of your life?

4. Write your own two-hundred-word obituary, describing what you hope your legacy might be—how will your friends remember you? Then pare this down to one hundred words as a way to get at what's most essential. If you're part of a writing group, try writing obituaries for each other; sometimes we need to be reminded of our gifts by those who know us well.

5. Write a haiku that you would like to be your epitaph. Employing this form will force you to be concise; don't worry that it can't capture everything significant about your life. Use it as an opportunity to remember that, as Mother Theresa said, "Each of us is merely a small instrument; all of us, after accomplishing our mission, will disappear."

Nineteen

Befriending Solitude and Grief

Loneliness is the poverty of self, solitude the richness of self.

—May Sarton, *Journal of a Solitude*

Brenda

I live alone, with my dog and my cat for company. Solitude has become a natural way of life for me, and most of the time it's fine. I enjoy my little routines, the freedom to just be myself at all hours. I enjoy the quiet. But sometimes it's not fine at all. Sometimes the quiet contentment of solitude veers into loneliness and despair; the line between the two is very thin indeed. May Sarton's *Journal of a Solitude*, published in 1973, was one of the first books to honestly, intimately glimpse the nature of being alone. I remember reading it as a young woman with the avid, breathless attention one might give to a thriller. She writes,

I am here alone for the first time in weeks to take up my "real" life again at last. That is what is strange—that friends, even passionate love, are not my real life unless there is time alone in which to explore and to discover what is happening or has happened. . . . I hope to break through into the rough, rocky depths, to the matrix itself. There is violence there and anger never resolved. My need to be alone is balanced against my fear of what will happen when suddenly I enter the huge empty silence if I cannot find support there.

Sarton, an accomplished poet, understood the necessity of being alone, but also apprehended the need for support in this endeavor—she knew the fear that can arise and choke us. And it's remarkably easy to go from content to miserable in an instant. When I'm writing well, I feel the blessing of solitude—which is, as one psychology journal puts it, "a state of being alone where you provide yourself wonderful and sufficient company." My writing becomes my "wonderful and sufficient company," but when my attention falters, when I devolve into indecision and fretting, loneliness takes over and nothing seems right.

While I know that we need to build our tolerance for alone time as writers, we also might need boundaries to that alone time. And we need the little rituals and routines that sustain us, that help keep our better minds on track.

William Stafford, a great poet, woke at 4 a.m. every morning to write a poem. He was alone for that hour, yes, but also in the deep presence of the world. In a beautiful essay called "My Father's Place," Stafford's son, Kim Stafford, writes of sleeping at his father's house a few days after the poet's death and being woken at his father's customary hour. "The house wanted me to rise," he writes. "There was a soft tug. Nothing mystical, just a habit to the place. The air was sweet, life was good, it was time."

So Kim rises in the dark, makes instant coffee and toast (his father's customary repast), and goes to the coach, lies down, places his head in the dent his father's head had made in the silk pillow after years of mornings just like this one. He is poised to write, but Kim does not write, not yet. Instead he allows himself to simply be in that room, with the spirit of his father, and to take in all the ordinary details: the curtains, the sunflowers in a vase, the pollen that has dropped from those sunflowers onto the table. He writes,

The pollen seemed to burn, so intense in color and purpose. But the house—the house didn't want me to write anything profound. The soft tug that had wakened me, the tug I still felt, wanted me to be there with myself, awake, awake to everything ordinary. . . . I remembered how my father had said once that such a time alone would allow anyone to go inward, in order to go outward. Paradoxically, he said, you had to go into yourself in order to find the patterns that were bigger than your own life. . . .

It's not about trying. It's not about writing poems. It's not about achievement, certainly not fame, importance. It's about being there exactly with the plain life of a time before first light, with breath, . . . about the worn silk, the blanket, and that little dusting of pollen from the sunflowers . . . there was this abundance in time and place and habit. And then I had a page, I closed my notebook, and I rose for the day. There was much to do, but I had done the big thing already.

I hope we can always be awake to ourselves, and find "abundance in time and place and habit." In the midst of solitude, we can feel our compatriots surrounding and supporting us. We can "go inward, in order to go outward." We can learn to feel that soft tug, that beckoning, and follow it with confidence.

Holly

I'm writing in a cottage in Ocean Park, on the Washington coast. It's no more than fifteen square feet but has everything I need: a bed, a couch, a small refrigerator, a tiny stove, and a round wooden table that serves as dining table and desk. The walls are painted mint green and lavender, all the furnishings are Salvation Army, so the cottage has a comfortable, broken-in feeling, each item with its story, its history. Built in the 1950s, the cottage has small wood-paned windows that look out onto a grassy courtyard where dogs gather and sniff each other, and where right now Fox is snoozing in the sun.

I came here this weekend with Fox to walk on the beach, read and write, and to let in the grief I've been holding at arm's length. My father died a few weeks ago, and there was so much to do just to get through each day—calling relatives, writing the obituary, planning the memorial service, sending letters to those who couldn't come. There's comfort in these actions—something to focus on—comfort from the community: the church ladies who served us turkey sandwiches, potato salad, and brownies, the neighbors who brought hot dishes and desserts, the endless writing of thank-you notes. But I'm alone now, trying to reenter my life, and the grief feels so much bigger than me. I know that this deeper letting go happens only when I'm in the presence of greater forces, like the ocean, and so I came here to walk the empty winter beaches.

I know how much I need solitude, though we all avoid it because it can so easily, as Brenda pointed out, spill over into loneliness. But I know it's only when I'm alone that I can listen for the still, quiet voice, even if that voice tells me what I may not want to hear or nudges me to face emotions that feel overwhelming.

This year has been filled with loss. Not only did my father die, but several months earlier, my beloved friend Rags passed away. During the weeks following his death, I set up an altar by my meditation cushion with candles, flowers, and photographs, and each morning I wrote Rags a letter, telling him what I saw on my walk, what conversation I overheard the day before, what small delight I encountered—a black fox on the trail, a book he'd like. These few minutes spent reaching across the mysterious vastness between us felt sacred, and slowly, over many weeks, the grief began to recede, replaced by gratitude for his presence in my life and the lives of so many who loved him. When my father died I did the same, wanting to keep his spirit close as long as I could.

I received many thoughtful condolence notes these past weeks, but one in particular encouraged me to embrace the grieving, not let the busyness of life push it away, reminding me how easy it is to avoid making time to be with grief and loss. Now that I'm here, I'm grateful I listened to this friend's advice. I'm especially grateful for friends who can be with you in grief, who don't tell you to put it behind you, to get over it, to get on with your life—friends who will sit beside you in sorrow.

Of course, the death of my father stirs up feelings of grief about losing my mother ten years earlier. As those who've lost both parents know, we're in the world in a different way then. It wasn't until a few years after my mother died that I was able to slow down and let the grief catch up with me. I couldn't face being alone then, but I somehow knew what I needed: to be alone but supported by a community. Serendipitously, the Mindfulness Community's Deer Park Monastery in California was just opening that year, and Thich Nhat Hanh would be in residence for several months over the summer. I signed up for a week and invited a good friend, who was just recovering from breast cancer, to join me. There, sitting in the new, spacious, light-filled hall on bamboo floors— the beautiful young nuns with their shaved heads sitting on cushions beside us, the gentle voices of Thich Nhat Hanh and Sister True Emptiness leading us in the morning chanting—I finally was able to let my tears of grief come.

Since then, I've felt the presence of my mother frequently and I trust that, at some point, my father's presence, too, will reappear. When my sisters and I gather together now, our time is filled with telling stories from our childhood. Never mind that we each remember the stories differently; what matters is that we're keeping our parents with us in memory. A friend once shared a story of when she was nine and asked her father what would happen to him when he died, and he replied, "I'll be with you as long as you remember me." This is what stories and poetry allow us to do, isn't it? Not only remember those we love, but re-inhabit our lives together for a moment.

In Tess Gallagher's essay "The Poem as a Reservoir for Grief," she points out how important it is to gain the wisdom of our grieving.

> Until individuals maintain a responsible relationship to their own losses and changes, there will be no such thing as a hopeful future. For, like the Taoist description of the wheel in terms of the strong, empty spaces *between* the spokes, one's future depends not only on the visible spokes of the present, but also on those invisible elements from the past—those things we are missing, are grieving for and which we have forgotten and left behind in order to recover them again as new meaning, new feeling.

For example, in her poem "Sixteenth Anniversary," Gallagher describes her annual ritual of retreating to a cabin at LaPush on the anniversary of her husband Raymond Carver's death. Note how she addresses Ray as if they are, indeed, together:

> If you were here we'd
> sit outside, accompanying
> the roar of waves
> as they mingle with the low notes
> of the buoy bell's plaintive warning,
> like some child blowing
> against the cold edge of a metal pipe.
> I'd tell you how the Quileute
> were transformed from wolves
> into people, though I'm unsure
> if they liked the change . . .

I'm looking for
the moon now. We'll have
something new
to say to each other.

On a visit just a few years ago, my father and I walked this beach together, so it's easy to imagine him beside me, walking slowly, his carved wooden walking stick—a gift from my sister—leaving a trail of ellipses in the soft sand. We're together again, my father and I, for a few moments with the wind and waves, re-inhabiting our memories.

I'm reminded again of the value of mindfulness practice: This grief may feel overwhelming, but we can be with it only in each moment. I'm grateful for my partner, John, and my sisters, as we support each other in remembering and letting go of my father. Yet, no matter how much support we receive, we still need to experience our grief alone, even if we're in the silent presence of others. May we find ways to befriend grief, solitude, and other difficult emotions—to welcome them, invite them in. Only then will we recover and grow from our losses, glean the truths they offer.

Contemplation Practices

1. What happens when you find yourself alone? Make a list of ways you provide yourself with "wonderful and sufficient company" even when alone. The next time you find yourself alone, do one item on that list.

2. Arrange for some "retreat" time, even if it's just an hour or two. For example, you can let your family know you're "on retreat" for a morning each

week to write. Or you might arrange to trade houses with a friend for an afternoon, ensuring fewer distractions. For longer writing retreats, check out the numerous writing colonies and retreat centers that exist precisely for this purpose.

Writing Practices

1. Write about a time that had the positive qualities of solitude. Write about a time where loneliness seemed more prevalent. Or write about both at the same time.

2. As a child, were you primarily alone or with others? Write a scene or image from your childhood that shows your propensity for either solitude or community.

3. Have you ever been in the presence of someone who is ill? This can be as simple as caring for a sick child or friend, or as extreme as caring for a dying parent, spouse, or friend. See if you can re-create a specific moment from this time, focusing on a small detail or image that stays with you. Allow yourself to suspend the moment, staying with it even if it's difficult, breathing in and out.

4. Write a letter to someone you've lost—a parent, grandparent, or friend— tell that person what you saw that day that reminded you of him or her—be specific.

5. Write a poem for someone you've lost in which you bring past and present experiences together, addressing the person as Tess Gallagher addresses Raymond Carver in "Sixteenth Anniversary."

Twenty

Balancing Contemplation and Action

> Peace is all around us. . . . It is not a matter of faith;
> it is a matter of practice.
>
> —Thich Nhat Hanh, *Touching Peace*

Brenda

I've spent the weekend at a meditation center in Seattle. The *sangha* members here have created a beautiful and powerful space for practice—with wide, rough wood beams across the ceiling, a polished wood floor beneath us, softly lit wall sconces, reed window shades that filter the light. A statue of Kuan Yin, the bodhisattva of compassion, adorns the altar. She sits with downturned gaze, her palm open to receive the suffering of the world with equanimity.

The center is located in a fairly rough neighborhood in south Seattle, an area that seems to be in transition. A boarded-up house with graffiti scrawled across its walls sits just across the street from new townhouses with burnished wood shingles, balconies, and gardens. In the middle of all this sits the practice center, and inside it we ring bells, sit, watch our breath, and walk slowly, the soles of our feet fully touching the ground with each step. We chant the morning sutras, we bow to one another, we eat a meal slowly in quiet mindfulness. Outside, we walk in a single-file line for a half hour on the winding paths through a small garden, and on each rotation I see something new: the small blue flowers on the rosemary bush; the waving fronds of milkweed; the bare branches of the fig tree, with a few small withered fruits still clinging to the limbs.

But mainly I look up and see the line of people, bundled in hats and coats and scarves, each one unique, yet each one of us bound by our common purpose here, walking mindfully on this path through a small garden together. We're walking in the early winter sun, and inside the cooks are making our lunch. Soon we'll be inside again, holding our bowls, ladling soup and rice, sitting together as we say the five contemplations. I'm not walking this path alone. We are walking this path together.

In a Dharma talk, our teacher, Eileen Kiera, told us a story that, for me, explained my central dilemma with contemplative practice: If we strive to be accepting of all that is, how does anything ever change? In this story, Eileen described the young Thich Nhat Hanh (also called "Thay" for short) in Vietnam. This was during the 1950s, a fractious time in a country just coming out of war with the French, a time of civil discord—the north dividing from the south. Thich Nhat Hanh and five friends retreated to the hills and built a small temple, a place of refuge.

There was a lake at this temple, covered in lotus blossoms. The lotus is a sturdy flower that grows out of the mud, blooming resplendently in the rot and decay. Its petals open at dawn and close at dusk, watertight, responsive to the fluctuations of the light. It is known as a symbol of purity, a manifestation of awakening.

Each evening, Thay and his friends would row out onto the lake and pour a little water into the center of each lotus flower, just as the petals were closing for the night. As the flowers began to open at dawn, the young monks would row out again—the lake quiet, flat, misty—and gather each bit of water into a kettle until they had enough for all six of them to drink. They heated this water in a little brazier in the bottom of the boat, added a little tea, and then drank mindfully together as the light came up over the hills.

I like to imagine it: six monks with shaved heads, plain robes, in a country torn by war, knowing that great action must happen, but must happen in its own way. Knowing that spending the time to gather water from lotus flowers, to sit quietly and drink tea made of this water, is just as important—perhaps more so—than any other action they can take in this moment. Knowing that, yes, they can make tea with any old water, and it would be fine, and they could drink it quickly and hold meetings, hammer out a plan. But these monks know better. Through a lifetime of practice, they know that water gathered patiently from the petals of the lotus will enhance not only the tea but the drinker of the tea. And they know that drinking this tea together as the dawn gives way to the day is the most important part of their time together.

The future will come. They will begin the School of Youth for Social Service, which will eventually send hundreds of members out into the countryside to do whatever needs doing. They will teach if teaching is needed. They will tend the sick if such tending is required. They will bring food, if food is in short supply. All of this will emerge from the simple act of monks sipping a cup of tea made sacred in their mindfulness.

Now, in my own house, the morning has come. My body stretches; the animals rise to greet me. I'm not drinking tea brewed from consecrated water, but the picture of those monks in their canoes stays with me. And I'm writing, which may be my own form of lotus watering.

I'd like to believe that in our best writing we pour what we have into cupped lotus flowers. We wait through the night as the water simmers inside the petals, transforming into something with power to truly sustain us. We rise at first light and gather what we can. And we must do this work together, in mindfulness,

rocking gently on the lake with no hope or expectation or plan for the future—
just waiting for the dawn to arrive.

Holly

The first day of the new year seems inordinately dark. Fox and I were up early to walk, and at 8 a.m., I'm still waiting for light to glimmer on the horizon. I'm aware of how much I want this day to be special, a fresh start in a new year. But right now the day just looks like any other Northwest winter day: gray, wet, drizzle. I light candles, plug in the white Christmas lights I've not yet taken down, put on the new Tingstad and Rumbel CD, *A Moment of Peace,* that my friend Anna gave me, and settle into the slow, rippling notes of the guitar and oboe.

What is this wish to turn over a new leaf with December's calendar page, the desire to begin anew somehow, in some small way, even if it's just resolving to remember to floss? But because this day calls for bigger changes, I find myself falling into my year-end habit of making lists with way too many resolutions. Personal behaviors head the list—meditate every morning, don't read email after 9 p.m., cut back on chocolate. Other challenges show up later—turn down the thermostat, drive less, take the bus more. By the end of the list, I'm already feeling overwhelmed, knowing only one or two will stick past the first few days.

Several years ago, I went on a four-day meditation retreat over New Year's at Cloud Mountain. By the end of four days of sitting and walking meditation, I'd returned to my body and I didn't need my mind to make lists of what I wanted to change; my body knew and didn't put up an argument. This is the challenge, isn't it? To work with the desire to change skillfully, to acknowledge the impulse to improve but not to become enslaved by it. To let the resolutions come from a deeper, quieter place, not from the stern taskmaster who delights in making lists, cracking the whip. And so I resolve (I know, I know, one more resolution!) to do so and, more importantly, to learn to tell the difference.

I'm encouraged in this effort by the example of friend and meditation teacher Kurt Hoelting. Several years ago, after watching the movie *An Inconvenient Truth,* Kurt decided to calculate his carbon footprint. What he found was revealing: Because he flies frequently to teach, his carbon footprint was bigger than he'd expected. Surprised to see this gap between his values—he is concerned about climate change—and his behavior—he's burning carbon due to his transportation habits—he made a conscious choice to spend a year living plane- and car-free. For that year he never went farther than one hundred kilometers from his home on Whidbey Island, traveling only by foot, paddle, and pedal.

On the winter solstice, he celebrated the end of his "year in circumference." A snowstorm kept us from joining him, so I visited his website to see if he'd posted any end-of-the-year reflections. What I found was heartening: Despite the snow, seventy-five people walked the half mile up a snowy driveway to the Whidbey Institute to celebrate with him. Here's an excerpt of what he said about his year choosing to live car-free:

- Staying close to home and actively exploring my home terrain has vastly increased my sense of connection and belonging in this place.
- My inner life feels richer and more grounded than it did a year ago.
- My sense of connection to my neighbors and gratitude for my community is much stronger.
- The daily act of moving from place to place is lived time now, rather than lost time. I'm not checked out when I'm traveling. I'm much more fully engaged.
- I am far less prone to seasonal depression and feelings of despair about the world. I am more open to the truth of what we face, without being so overwhelmed by it.

~ I am much more willing to share my gifts and talents without the burden of feeling that my actions are continually out of alignment with my deepest values and convictions.

~ I'm far more hopeful that serious change is possible, that we each have it in us to make real changes on a scale commensurate with the challenges we face.

This list reminds me of the workshop Kurt and I taught last fall at the North Cascades Institute, when Kurt was winding up his "year in circumference." We had just finished our last session together, in which we talked about how, as writers, we can bear witness for nature and what that might mean. We acknowledged that bearing witness can feel heavy, carrying all our grief for the destruction of the earth we love. But we shared how bearing witness can be joyful, too, how witnessing can be an act of praise. Kurt reminded us that we'll be effective only if our actions come from joy, not from fear and guilt. He chose to undertake his car-free year not as a sacrifice, but as a choice he made that can—and did—bring its own kind of pleasure.

At the end, we posed these questions: How might you bridge the gap between what you love and how you live your life? What small actions might you take to enable you to live in alignment with your deepest values?

When we reassembled, we sat quietly in silence. Then Kurt opened the discussion. "Just throw in a small pebble," he suggested. One participant, Francis, told us she planned to begin walking around her neighborhood to get to know it, and because she enjoyed the singing we had done together the night before, she hoped to find a group of people who would like to combine walking with singing. Jordana planned to water the seeds of good works already under way: She gave the example of Microsoft composting in its cafeterias and how she might help develop "best practices" that could be taken to other corporations.

Kathy planned to make room for meditation in her too-busy life, to keep space clear for her inner work.

Alone, the challenges we all face feel daunting: climate change, species extinction, the accelerating pace of our lives that leaves so little time for spirit, for contemplation. But together, in our circle, writing and talking about it, it felt less overwhelming, more possible to choose just one action, one small pebble to toss into the circle. We trusted that the ripples would extend outward as we returned to our daily lives, mindful of Thomas Merton's reminder to "not neglect the silence at our core."

As we bring our actions into alignment with our deepest values, we free ourselves. As Kathleen Dean Moore and Michael P. Nelson, the editors of *Moral Ground: Ethical Action for a Planet in Peril*, write, "The odd fact is that those lifeways that are most destructive of the world often turn out to be exactly those lifeways that are most destructive of the spirit. You'll know you are achieving integrity when you are surprised by happiness and the unexpected joy of freedom." Reading this, I'm reminded that as we work to protect our spirits, we free ourselves to protect the world, that contemplation and action are, like a Möbius strip, inextricably connected. I'm also reminded that because the problems we face are so complex, we need to think carefully as we move into action.

Every moment can be the start of a new year. May we remember to make resolutions from a deeper place, resolutions that arise from joy rather than guilt, that balance contemplation with action. Through reading, writing, and contemplative practice, alone and together, we can support each other in aligning our actions with our values, allowing ourselves space and energy to commit to the larger work of the world.

Contemplation Practices

1. The next time you pick up your pen or go to your computer, take a deep breath. Consider the story of Thich Nhat Hanh and his monks, gathering sacred water from the lotus petals. Imagine your own metaphor for how writing can be a sacred act. When do you feel most peaceful? How can you translate this peace into great action?

2. Gather several friends to reflect on these questions: Is there a gap between your values and how you live your life? How could you bridge that gap? What small actions might you take to enable you to live in alignment with your deepest values? Share your reflections, then support each other in finding ways to live in closer alignment with your values. Pay attention to how even small actions allow you to feel more free and encourage you to take larger actions.

3. Consider how your writing interest and skills might be used in service of a social justice issue or other greater purpose. For example, led by Northwest poet Sam Hamill, many poets have used their writing to take a stand against war (poetsagainstthewar.org) or for peace (newpoetsforpeace.com). Another Northwest poet, Kelli Russell Agodon, put out a call for submissions and assembled a broadside series called "The Making of Peace" that traveled to thirty-seven states (www.agodon.com/themakingofpeace).

Writing Practices

1. Make a list of all the resolutions your conscious mind wants you to make. Then set the list aside and meditate for ten minutes. Next, pick up a pencil and make a new list. Are the resolutions the same or different? Which are you more motivated to carry out?

2. In a book group, or with a group of friends, read Kurt Hoelting's *The Circum-ference of Home: One Man's Yearlong Quest for a Radically Local Life.* Inspired by his action to spend a year living car-free, reflect on what actions you might take in your life to live in closer alignment with your values. Write these down, then share them with the group and commit to choosing one action. Keep a journal—or write a blog—documenting how this action creates a greater sense of integrity and freedom.

3. In an essay called "The Inner Climate," Pico Iyer makes a compelling case that we need to address not just the outer landscape of climate change but our "inner landscape" as well, emphasizing the importance of contempla-tive practice. After reading the excerpt from his essay below, write your own essay in response.

> Our outer environment can only begin to be healed by our inner, and I'm not sure we can ever truly tend to our polluted waters, our shrink-ing forests, the madness we've loosed on the air until we begin to try to clean up the inner waters, and attend to the embattled wild spaces within us. Action without reflection is what got us into this mess in the first place, and the only answer is not action, but, first, clearer reflection. A peace treaty signed by men who are still territorial, jeal-ous, or unquiet—Jerusalem tells me this—is not going to create any real peace at all. A commitment to the environment based only on what is outside of us forgets that the source of our problems—and solutions—is invisible, and that "nature" is a word we apply to what's within as well as without.

A Final Offering

Poems would be easy if our heads weren't so full of the day's clatter. The task is to get through to the other side, where we can hear the deep rhythms that connect us with the stars and the tides.

—Stanley Kunitz, *Collected Poems*

We began this book with Denise Levertov's poem describing the longing to be "a bell awakened," and now that we have reached the end, we feel the reverberations of that bell echoing throughout the pages. We hope you have found some insights into your own writing process, some tools that might help you to create more space in your life for contemplation and writing, and ways to create a community that supports you in this endeavor. We encourage you to continue on with the quest to, as Kunitz puts it, "get through to the other side, where we can hear the deep rhythms that connect us with the stars and the tides."

The poem "You Reading This, Be Ready," by William Stafford, encapsulates, for us, many of the concepts we've introduced in this book. He wrote the poem in his customary way—on the couch in his study in the early morning hours—a few days before his death. The reader is addressed in the very title, and so we seem to be in the room, breathing with him in this spacious quietude. We offer this poem to you as our closing bell.

You Reading This, Be Ready

Starting here, what do you want to remember?
How sunlight creeps along a shining floor?
What scent of old wood hovers, what softened
sound from outside fills the air?

Will you ever bring a better gift for the world
than the breathing respect that you carry
wherever you go right now? Are you waiting
for time to show you some better thoughts?

When you turn around, starting here, lift this
new glimpse that you found; carry into evening
all that you want from this day. This interval you spent
reading or hearing this, keep it for life—

What can anyone give you greater than now,
starting here, right in this room, when you turn around?

Bibliography

Here are the sources for many of the readings referred to in this book, both in the chapters and exercises, that you can find in your local bookstore or library. We hope you will continue to read works that help you access your own contemplative writing mind.

Ackerman, Diane. *A Natural History of the Senses*. Random House, 1990.

Andrew, Elizabeth Jarrett. *On the Threshold: Home, Hardwood, & Holiness*. Westview, 2005.

———. *Writing the Sacred Journey: The Art and Practice of Spiritual Memoir*. Skinner House Books, 2005.

Bishop, Elizabeth. *The Complete Poems, 1927–1979*. Farrar, Straus and Giroux, 1984.

Cameron, Julia. *The Artist's Way*, 10th ed. Tarcher/Putnam, 2002.

Christman, Jill. "The Sloth." *Brevity 26* (Winter 2008).

Chuang-Tzu. *The Way of Chuang-Tzu*, 2nd ed. Ed. and transl. Thomas Merton. New Directions, 2010.

Collins, Billy. *Picnic, Lightning*. University of Pittsburgh, 1998.

Didion, Joan. *Slouching Toward Bethlehem*. Farrar, Straus and Giroux, 2008.

Doty, Mark. *Sweet Machine: Poems.* Harper Perennial, 1998.

Dubus, Andre, III, and Philip Zaleski, eds. *The Best Spiritual Writing, 2001.* Harper, 2001.

Duncan, David James. *River Teeth: Stories and Writing.* The Dial Press, 1996.

Eliot, T. S. *Collected Poems, 1909–1962.* Harcourt Brace Jovanovich, 1991.

Fiffer, Sharon, and Steve Fiffer. *Body.* Harper Perennial, 2000.

Gallagher, Tess. *A Concert of Tenses.* University of Michigan, 1987.

———. *Dear Ghosts: Poems.* Graywolf, 2008.

Gensei. *Grass Hill: Poetry and Prose by the Japanese Monk Gensei.* Translated by Burton Watson. Columbia University Press, 1983.

Goldberg, Natalie. *Writing Down the Bones: Freeing the Writer Within*, expanded ed. Shambhala, 2010.

Green, Samuel. *The Grace of Necessity.* Carnegie Mellon University Press, 2008.

Gregg, Linda. *The Sacraments of Desire.* Graywolf, 1991.

Gulyas, Lee. "Entering the Kingdom of Invertebrates." *Isotope: A Journal of Literary Nature and Science Writing*, Vol. 6.2 (Fall/Winter 2008).

Gunderson, David. "Meal Gatha." *Earthlight Magazine*, Vol. 14, No. 1 (Spring 2004).

Hamill, Sam, ed. *Poets against the War.* Nation Books, 2003.

Hass, Robert. *Praise.* Ecco, 1999.

Herring, Laraine. *Writing Begins with the Breath: Embodying Your Authentic Voice.* Shambhala, 2007.

Hirshfield, Jane. *The Lives of the Heart.* Harper Perennial, 1997.

Hoelting, Kurt. *The Circumference of Home: One Man's Yearlong Quest for a Radically Local Life.* DaCapo Press, 2010.

Housden, Roger. *Ten Poems to Change Your Life.* Harmony, 2001.

Hopkins, Gerard Manley. *Poems and Prose.* Penguin Classics, 1985.

Hughes, Holly. *Boxing the Compass.* Floating Bridge, 2007.

————. "Hidden." *Alaska Quarterly Review*, Vol. 24, Nos. 1 & 2 (Spring & Summer 2007).

Jackson, Maggie. *Distracted: The Erosion of Attention and the Coming Dark Age.* Prometheus, 2009.

Kenyon, Jane. *Otherwise: New and Selected Poems.* Graywolf, 1996.

Kingsolver, Barbara. *Small Wonder: Essays.* Harper Perennial, 2003.

Kunitz, Stanley. *The Collected Poems.* W.W. Norton & Co., 2002.

Kurtz, Glenn. *Practicing: A Musician's Return to Music.* Vintage, 2008.

Kuusisto, Stephen. *Planet of the Blind.* Delta, 1998.

Lamott, Anne. *Traveling Mercies: Some Thoughts on Faith.* Anchor, 2000.

Lee, Li-Young. *Rose.* BOA, 1993.

Levertov, Denise. *Breathing the Water.* New Directions, 1987

————. *Selected Poems,* New Directions, 2003.

Lindberg, Anne Morrow. *Gift from the Sea.* Pantheon Books, 1991.

Max, Lin. "The Piemaker." In *Claiming the Spirit Within: A Sourcebook of Women's Poetry,* ed. Marilyn Sewell. Beacon Press, 2001.

McClahanan, Rebecca. "Early Morning, Downtown 1 Train." *Georgia Review* (Summer 2009).

————. "Signs and Wonders." In *Short Takes: Brief Encounters with Contemporary Nonfiction,* ed. Judith Kitchen. W.W. Norton, 2005.

Merwin, W. S. *Migration: New and Selected Poems.* Copper Canyon, 2007.

Miller, Brenda. *Listening Against the Stone.* Skinner House Books, 2011.

————. *Season of the Body: Essays.* Sarabande Books, 2002.

Moore, Kathleen Dean, and Michael P. Nelson, eds. *Moral Ground: Ethical Action for a Planet in Peril.* Trinity University Press, 2011.

Nhat Hanh, Thich. *Fragrant Palm Leaves: Journals, 1962–1966.* Riverhead Trade, 1999.

————. *The Miracle of Mindfulness: An Introduction to the Practice of Meditation.* Beacon Press, 1999.

————. *The Heart of the Buddha's Teaching.* Three Rivers Press, 1999.

————. "The Moment is Perfect." *Shambhala Sun* (May 2008).

————. *Peace Is Every Step: The Path of Mindfulness.* Bantam, 1992.

————. *Present Moment, Wonderful Moment,* 2nd ed. Parallax Press, 2006.

———. *Touching Peace: Practicing the Art of Mindful Living*, revised ed. Parallax Press, 2009.

Tippett, Krista. *On Being*. American Public Media podcast.

O'Reilley, Mary Rose. *The Garden at Night: Burnout and Breakdown in the Teaching Life*. Heineman, 2005.

Pagh, Nancy. *After.* Floating Bridge, 2008.

Perillo, Lucia. *The Body Mutinies.* Purdue University, 1996.

Piercy, Marge. *The Moon Is Always Female.* Knopf, 1980.

Pyle, Robert Michael. *Walking the High Ridge: Life as Field Trip.* Milkweed, 2000.

Rilke, Rainier Maria. *Selected Poems of Rainier Maria Rilke,* transl. Robert Bly. Harper Perennial, 1981.

Rogers, Pattiann. *Eating Bread and Honey.* Milkweed, 1997.

Rumi, Jalal al-Din. *The Essential Rumi*, transl. Coleman Barks. HarperOne, 2004.

Sarton, May. *Journal of a Solitude.* W. W. Norton, 1992.

Shumaker, Peggy. *Just Breathe Normally.* Bison Books, 2009.

Solnit, Rebecca. *A Field Guide to Getting Lost.* Penguin, 2006.

Snyder, Gary. "Writers and the War against Nature." In *The Best American Spiritual Writing 2007,* ed. Philip Zaleski. Houghton Mifflin, 2007.

Stafford, Kim. *Early Morning: Remembering My Father, William Stafford.* Graywolf, 2003.

———. *The Muses Among Us: Eloquent Listening and Other Pleasures of the Writer's Craft.* University of Georgia, 2003.

Stafford, William. *The Way It Is: New and Selected Poems.* Graywolf, 1999.

Suiter, John, ed. *Poets on the Peaks: Gary Snyder, Phillip Whalen & Jack Kerouac in the Cascades, 2002.* Counterpoint, 2002.

Sund, Robert. *Poems from Ish River Country.* Counterpoint, 2005.

Teshigahara Sofu. *Kadensho: The Book of Flowers,* Sogetsu Shuppan, 1996.

Tharp, Twyla. *The Creative Habit: Learn It and Use It for Life.* Simon and Schuster, 2005.

Thomas, Abigail. *Safekeeping: Some True Stories from a Life.* Anchor, 2001.

———. *A Three Dog Life: A Memoir.* Harvest Books, 2007.

Thoreau, Henry David. *Walden; or, Life in the Woods.* Dover, 1995.

To the Best of Our Knowledge. Public Radio International podcast.

Unamuno, Miguel de. "Throw Yourself Like Seed," transl. Robert Bly. In *Roots & Wings: Poetry from Spain 1900–1975*, White Pine Press, 2005.

White, E. B. *Charlotte's Web.* HarperCollins, 2004.

Williams, Terry Tempest. *Refuge.* Vintage, 1992.

Writer's Almanac, The, with Garrison Keillor. National Public Radio. http://writersalmanac.publicradio.org.

Acknowledgments

A book like this cannot be written by two people alone; it is the result of years of support and generous wisdom from the larger community. We give a deep bow of gratitude to the people and places that were instrumental during our writing process:

The Venerable Thich Nhat Hanh and the monks and nuns at Deer Park Monastery;

Dharmacayra Eileen Kiera, Roshi Jack Duffy, and the Mountain Lamp Community;

The Bellingham Mindfulness Community and the Mindfulness Community of Puget Sound;

Yoga teacher Michal Retter and the yoginis at Inner Composure Yoga;

Stan Rubin and Judith Kitchen, co-directors of the Rainier Writers Workshop (RWW) at Pacific Lutheran University, where this project was conceived, and all the faculty members of RWW, whose lively conversations on collaboration helped shape this project;

Arthur Whiteley, Kathy Cowell, and all the staff of the Helen Riaboff Whiteley Center at Friday Harbor, where many of the early drafts of this book were written in Dixy's Study;

Cottages at Hedgebrook, where we worked together in the Meadow House, refining our vision;

Mark and Teru Lundsten, who offered their guesthouse as a midway writing retreat;

Sheila Bender and the subscribers to her online magazine, *Writing It Real*, who provided valuable feedback on early chapters;

Nancy Canyon and Katie Humes, who provided writing support and feedback on early drafts;

Students in the Fishtrap Summer 2010 "Poetry as Practice, Poetry as Witness" workshop, who field-tested early chapters and exercises;

Staff at the North Cascades Institute, who provided a marvelous place for refuge and learning, and the students in the "Sit, Walk, Write" workshop who, along with co-teacher Kurt Hoelting, participated in early versions of these exercises;

Charles Claassen of the Book Fare Café, who provided many hearty bowls of soup during revisions;

Our respective institutions, Western Washington University and Edmonds Community College, for providing funding and professional development leave as we developed this book;

Mary Benard, editor extraordinaire at Skinner House Books, who was instrumental in shaping this book; and editor Marshall Hawkins, who patiently shepherded it into print;

John Pierce, for his good editorial sense (and for feeding us fava-feta tapenade);

And finally, all who support us, individually or together, too many to name: You know who you are.

We gratefully acknowledge permission to reprint the following:

Excerpt from "The Moose" from *The Complete Poems 1927–1979* by Elizabeth Bishop, copyright © 1979, 1983 by Alice Helen Methfessel, reprinted by permission of Farrar, Straus and Giroux, LLC.; excerpts from "Shoveling Snow with Buddha" from *Picnic, Lightning*, by Billy Collins, © 1998, reprinted by permission of the University of Pittsburgh Press; excerpt from "Throw Yourself Like Seed," by Miguel de Unamuno, translated by Robert Bly, from *Roots & Wings: Poetry from Spain 1900–1975*, published by White Pine Press, 2005, whitepine.org, reprinted with permission from White Pine Press; "Golden Retrievals" from *Sweet Machine* by Mark Doty, copyright © 1998 by Mark Doty, reprinted by permission of HarperCollins Publishers; Tess Gallagher, excerpt from "Sixteenth Anniversary" from *Midnight Lantern: New and Selected Poems*, copyright © 2011 by Tess Gallagher, reprinted by permission of The Permissions Company, Inc., on behalf of Graywolf Press, Minneapolis, Minnesota, www.graywolfpress.org; excerpt from "Poem Without a Category," from *Grass Hill: Poetry and Prose by the Japanese Monk Gensei* by Gensei, translated by Burton Watson, copyright © 1983 Columbia University Press, reprinted with permission of the publisher; Samuel Green, "April 9," "Sept. 9," "Sept. 11," and excerpt from "Sept. 14" from *The Grace of Necessity*, copyright © 2002, 2008 by Samuel Green, reprinted with the permission of The Permissions Company, Inc., on behalf of Carnegie Mellon University Press, www.cmu.edu/universitypress; Linda Gregg, "Glistening" from *All of It Singing: New and Selected Poems*, © 1991 by Linda Gregg, reprinted by permission of The Permissions Company, Inc., on behalf of Graywolf Press, Minneapolis, Minnesota, www.graywolfpress.org; excerpt from "Entering the Kingdom of Invertebrates" by Lee Gulyas from *Isotope: A Journal of Literary Science and Nature Writing*, reprinted with permission from author; "Meal Gatha" by David Gunderson was published in *Earthlight* magazine, Vol. 14.1, Spring 2004 and is used by permission of the author; four lines of "Santa Lucia" from *Praise* by Robert Hass, copyright © 1979 by Robert Hass, reprinted by permission of HarperCollins Publishers; "Salt Heart" (12 l.), "Three Foxes by the Edge of the Field at Twilight" (20 l.) from *The Lives of the Heart* by Jane Hirschfield, copyright © 1997 by Jane Hirschfield, reprinted by permission of HarperCollins Publishers; Jane Kenyon, "Otherwise" from *Collected Poems*, copyright © 2005 by The Estate of Jane Kenyon, reprinted by permission of The Permissions Company, Inc., on behalf of Graywolf Press, Minneapolis, Minnesota, www.graywolfpress.org; Li-Young Lee, "Eating Together" from *Rose*, copyright © 1986 by Li-Young Lee, reprinted with the permission of The Permissions Company, Inc., on behalf of BOA Editions, Ltd., www.boaeditions.org; "Variation